MONSTERS AND MAYHEM

IN CROSS-STITCH

Designs & Instructions for 25 Creatures & Cryptids

MONSTERS AND MAYHEM

IN CROSS-STITCH

Designs & Instructions for 25 Creatures & Cryptids

Designs and Artwork by Nicole LaBranche
Written by April LaBranche

SCHIFFER
CRAFT

4880 Lower Valley Road • Atglen, PA 19310

Other Schiffer Craft Books on Related Subjects:

PixlPeople: Cross-Stitch Your Favorite People, John-Michael Stoof, ISBN 978-0-7643-6191-3

Fables & Fairy Tales to Cross Stitch: French Charm for Your Stitchwork, Véronique Enginger, ISBN 978-0-7643-5478-6

Stitch with One Line: 33 Easy-to-Embroider Minimalist Designs, Martina Unterfrauner and Nuray Hatun, ISBN 978-0-7643-6758-8

Copyright © 2025 by Nicole LaBranche and April LaBranche

Library of Congress Control Number: 2024953132

Stitchers:
Caitlin "Cat" Booth: Goblin #1, Pegasus
Jen Hogan: Dragon
April LaBranche: Gnomes, Yeti
Marsha LaBranche: Bigfoot, Minotaur
Nicole LaBranche: Cerberus, Cyclops, Cthulhu, Gargoyle, Fairy,
    Jackalope, Mothman, Phoenix
Caroline Schleimer: Lake Monster
Deanna Simmons: Merpeople
Lily Stricklin: Unicorns
Leia Verner: Pegasus
Victoria Wisinski: Goblin #2, Kraken

Designed by Michael Douglas
Cover design by Lindsay Hess
Type set in Brandon Grotesque / Citrus Gothic / Corporate E Pro

ISBN: 978-0-7643-6961-2
ePub: 978-1-5073-0622-2
Printed in China
10 9 8 7 6 5 4 3 2 1

Published by Schiffer Craft
An imprint of Schiffer Publishing, Ltd.
4880 Lower Valley Road
Atglen, PA 19310
Phone: (610) 593-1777; Fax: (610) 593-2002
Email: Info@schifferbooks.com
Web: www.schifferbooks.com

For our complete selection of fine books on this and related subjects, please visit our website at www.schifferbooks.com. You may also write for a free catalog.

Schiffer Publishing's titles are available at special discounts for bulk purchases for sales promotions or premiums. Special editions, including personalized covers, corporate imprints, and excerpts, can be created in large quantities for special needs. For more information, contact the publisher.

We are always looking for people to write books on new and related subjects. If you have an idea for a book, please contact us at proposals@schifferbooks.com.

*This book is dedicated
to my familiar pup, Max,
who left us too soon
during the creation of this book.
We named the
Gargoyle for him.*

CONTENTS

23

27

39

43

49

61

65

69

83

87

93

INTRODUCTION

Welcome to our book of Monsters & Mayhem! It has been quite a journey for us, and we are so glad you have chosen to join us. In the following pages you will meet some unusual characters, read some interesting lore, and, most importantly, stitch some cool monsters!

Our characters and designs are based on legends and myths from around the world. We didn't take ourselves too seriously with the lore, since different places often have different interpretations of the legends.

We also tried to mix up the difficulty a little among the pieces. None of the designs are too difficult, but, while some are simple pieces with just a few colors, others are larger and require more colors and more counting!

We certainly hope that whether you're seasoned stitcher or a newbie, you can find something fun to love stitching our characters. And who knows, maybe you will learn something new as well!

What You Will Need

FABRIC

There are many types of fabric that can be used for cross-stitch, but the most common is called Aida fabric. Aida comes in a few different "counts." The count is the number of stitches, or X's, per inch. So 14 count Aida fabric means there are 14 stitches per inch, 16 count means 16 stitches, and so on. The higher the stitch count, the more stitches per inch, and the smaller your finished design will be. All our patterns call for 14 count aida.

TIP: Once you are more familiar with cross-stitching, try different fabric stitch counts. You may find you prefer stitching on a higher or lower stitch count.

To figure out what size your pieces of fabric should be for the pattern you are stitching, divide the number of stitches in one direction by the stitch count of the fabric.

For example: If a design is 70 stitches wide by 98 stitches long and you are stitching on a piece of Aida that is 14 count, you would divide 70 by 14, which equals 5 (70 ÷ 14 = 5), and you would divide 98 by 14, which equals 7 (98 ÷ 14 = 7), so your design will measure 5" × 7".

This is not the size of your fabric, however, since you will want to have extra fabric around your design to allow for framing. It's usually recommended to leave three or more inches of fabric around your design on all sides. So for our example, 5" + 3" + 3" = 11" and 7" + 3" + 3" = 13". This means that for your 5" × 7" design, you will want a piece of fabric that is 11" × 13".

THREAD

The most commonly used thread for cross-stitch is from a company called DMC. The thread color numbers listed on our patterns use the DMC color-coding system. If you'd like to use a different brand of thread, search for a color conversion website online. Enter the DMC number listed on the pattern, and the website will give you the corresponding color for the brand you'd like to use.

Cross-stitch thread, or floss, comes in a skein. Each skein is about 8 yards long, and the floss consists of six individual threads. We will be using two of the six threads at a time for the cross-stitches and two threads at a time for any backstitch.

TIP: As you gain more experience, you may find you prefer to use more threads, especially with a lower-count fabric. Using three threads instead of two on 14- or 16-count fabric can give you a fuller stitch.

NEEDLE

Most of the cross-stitch world will swear that #24 tapestry needles are the only good choice for working on 14-count Aida. These tapestry needles have a large eye for threading and a blunt tip. We, however, prefer sharper #6 embroidery needles for our pieces. We live life on the edge. As a beginner, you too may prefer the #24 tapestry needles since, with the blunt tip, you are less likely to draw blood. The choice is yours.

HOOP OR CLAMP FRAME

As with all cross-stitch supplies, there are many types of hoops and frames you can use for stitching. Most stitchers start out using a traditional wooden embroidery hoop to stitch. Some people come to prefer using C-clamp plastic frames or roll frames. We recommend starting with wood hoops, since they are easier to find and less expensive, and can make a nice frame for your piece when it is completed.

We always recommend shopping at your local small businesses before hitting the big-name stores for supplies.

Ready to get started?

A Quick How-To

GETTING STARTED

To start, let's find the center of your fabric. All our creature patterns are designed to be started in the center and stitched outward. If you'd rather start somewhere other than the center, you can either count the stitches out from the center starting point or measure the distance with a ruler. Remember that your fabric count is stitches per inch.

The easiest way to find the center of your fabric is to fold it once lengthwise and then again widthwise. Mark the center of the folds with an erasable fabric marker or a straight pin. That is your center!

Now to find the center of the pattern. The pattern center may be marked by the designer in different ways. Some mark the center stitch with a dot or arrow, and some designate the two grid lines that will cross in the center by making them a different color, usually red. Our patterns have red lines, and where those lines cross is the center of the pattern. The center of the pattern will correspond to the center you marked on your fabric.

Let's get you all hooped up and thread that needle! Loosen your hoop via the metal screw and remove the interior ring. Lay your fabric over the interior ring, making sure the center of your fabric is centered over the ring. Push the outer ring over the interior ring and fabric and tighten with the screw. Tighten the screw slowly while pulling your fabric lightly and evenly around the hoop, until it's taut. You don't want to pull too hard or too much in any one direction or your fabric may become misshapen. Don't worry if your hoop is too small to fully fit your piece, because you can remove the fabric from the hoop and move it around as needed. Your hoop will need to fit the full piece only if you intend to use it for framing.

Now, cut a piece of floss from your skein that is about 12 to 18 inches long (or the length of your forearm if you are bad at estimating length). Separate the six threads into the thread count noted on the pattern, usually two, and set the rest aside. Thread your needle with the two strands, but don't make any knots! We will instead secure the thread by stitching over the tail.

You can also find informational videos on our website at spotyourcolors. com/pages/how-to-cross-stitch.

GETTING STITCHIN'

Time to get stitchin'!

There are two main cross-stitch methods. The first method is to work a row of half X's (/ / /), then work back (\ \ \) to complete the X's *(see figure A)*. This method is used for most stitching. For these stitches you bring your

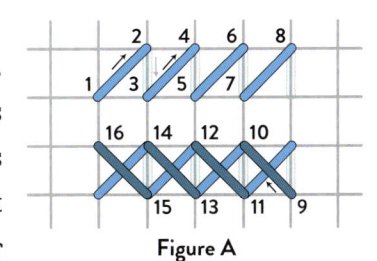

Figure A

needle up from the back of your fabric at point 1, down at point 2, up at point 3, down at point 4, and so forth until you have completed that row of stitches at point 8, then stitch back in the opposite direction, starting up from the back at 9, down at 10, up at 11, and so forth. The number of stitches in your line will depend on the pattern. Each stitch/X represents one square on your pattern.

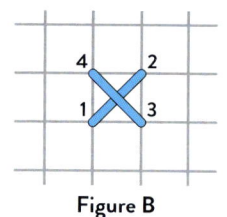

Figure B

The second method is to complete each X as you go *(see figure B)*. This method works better for vertical lines of stitches. In this instance you would bring your needle up from the back at point 1, down at point 2, up at point 3, and down at point 4, completing one full stitch.

It is important that all the X's are crossed in the same direction. If the X's are in varying directions, your finished piece may look funky or uneven. Try to keep even tension on your thread as you stitch. This will keep your stitches nice and neat and not distort your fabric.

In order for your finished design to lie flat, it is best to avoid knots on the back of the fabric. When you begin stitching, bring the threaded needle up from the back of the fabric and leave about a 1-inch tail of thread behind the fabric. Hold it in place with your finger while you stitch several stitches over the tail to lock it in place. Clip off any excess tail thread. When it's time to end your stitching, weave your needle through the last five or six stitches on the backside of the fabric and clip off the excess thread. Make sure you end your

stitching before you run your thread too short, or it can be difficult to run the needle under the last several stitches. If you find you have run your thread too short, you can simply undo several stitches to allow for enough thread to complete the securing. Pick up where you left off with your next length of thread.

Backstitch is the stitch sometimes used for outlines and details *(see figures C & D)*. For this stitch, your needle would come up

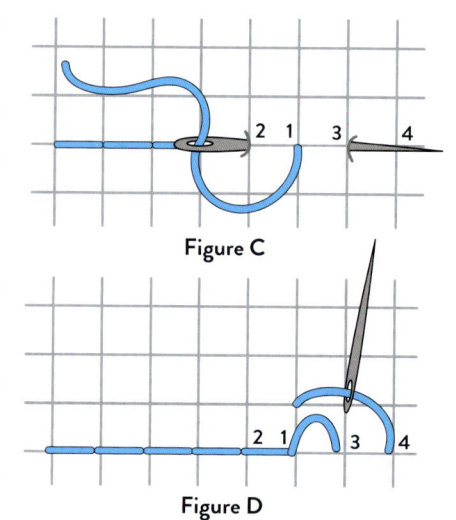

Figure C

Figure D

from behind your fabric at point 1, down at point 2. Then for the following stitch, you come back up at 3, back down at 1. And, for the third stitch, you come up at 4 and back down at 3. It may look a bit confusing, but don't let it scare you—it's easy once you get the hang of it!

FINISHING

If you need to clean your finished piece, remove it from the hoop and gently hand-wash in cool water, using a mild liquid detergent. Make sure to rinse your piece well. DO NOT WRING but, rather, place your piece flat on a clean, dry towel and roll it up to absorb excess water. Lay it flat to fully dry.

> TIP: Wooden embroidery hoops can also be painted or wrapped with fabric to give your finished piece a little something extra.

If you'd like to iron your piece, do so by placing it between two clean towels and pressing it with a warm iron. Ironing the piece between two towels will keep the iron from flattening your stitches. You can iron your piece while it's still damp, or after it's dry.

Once your piece has dried, it can be framed. To frame it with a wooden embroidery hoop, simply position it evenly within the two rings. Once it's secured and tightened, you can trim off all excess fabric and hang as is or leave about an inch of fabric all around, tuck the fabric behind the piece, and cover the back with other decorative fabric or felt. Additional methods of finishing can be found online; there are many!

FAIRY

NAME: Cordellia

AGE: Unknown

LOCATION: Redwood National Park, California, USA

HOBBIES: Stealing shiny things, gathering with friends,
shape-shifting, collecting pollen

The term Fairy, or Fae, can be used in reference to many mythological creatures. Most commonly it is used to refer to small humanoid beings with colorful wings and magical powers. These kinds of Fairies are neither good nor bad in relation to humans but are often believed to protect certain areas or landscapes, since they share a close bond with the earth. Some people believe Fairies to be tricksters, though not in a malevolent fashion, and view their hijinks as more an annoying inconvenience than anything else.

STRANDS USED:	2
AIDA COUNT:	14 (white)
HOOP SIZE:	4" (10 cm)
FINISHED SIZE:	3¼" × 3" (8 × 7.5 cm)
FRAMED SIZE:	4" × 4" (10 × 10 cm)

FAIRY Stitch Pattern

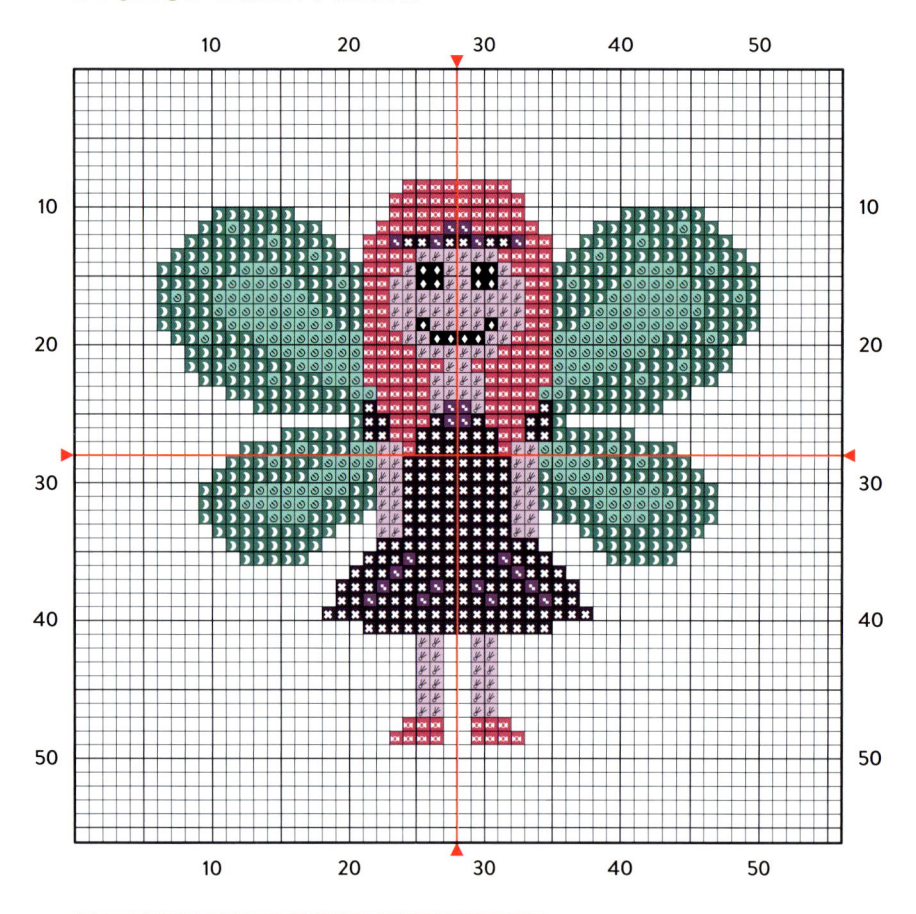

Often confused, Fairies and Sprites are considered different types of Fae. While both are small and magical, Fairies tend to be humanoid, while Sprites tend to resemble the fauna of the landscape they are protecting.

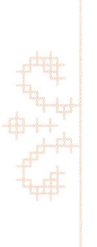 

It is said that in order to attract fairies to a garden, one should allow or encourage moss to grow freely. On the contrary, to repel fairies, one should grow St. John's wort or yarrow.

In 1917, two young girls, Elsie Wright and Frances Griffiths, became famous after taking a series of photographs showing themselves playing with various fairies. Sir Arthur Conan Doyle, believing the photographs to be real, used them in an article as proof of the supernatural. Though considered to be one of the greatest hoaxes of the 20th century, the photos are still believed by some people to be authentic.

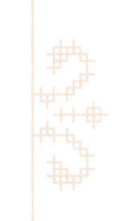

GNOMES

NAMES: Blarth and Betty

AGE: Unknown

LOCATION: Currently have a little hut in
Bloomfield, New Jersey, USA

HOBBIES: Gardening (obviously); moving swiftly through
the soil; bringing good luck to farmers, gardeners, and
other protectors and growers of the earth

Most modern-day depictions of Gnomes are of intelligent, miniature old men with long white beards in colorful pointed hats. They are usually depicted as doing yard work in or around someone's garden or flowerbeds. This version is generally referred to as a Garden Gnome. Other modern depictions differ, depending on the country. In the past, however, Gnomes have been portrayed in many ways, often far less humanoid and more like small goblins. All Gnomes are believed to be magical creatures that protect the forest and wildlife therein.

STRANDS USED:	2
AIDA COUNT:	14 (white)
HOOP SIZE:	4" (10 cm)
FINISHED SIZE:	3¾" × 3¾" (9.5 × 9.5 cm)
FRAMED SIZE:	4" × 4" (10 × 10 cm)

GNOMES Stitch Pattern

DMC Floss

◆ 310	R 666	↻ 898
312	701	Ecru
437	415	444

Gnomes are said to kiss each other by rubbing their noses together.

The oldest Garden Gnome statue in the world is Lampy, the Lamport Gnome. Though he travels extensively, he resides mostly at Lamport Hall in Lamport, England. He is the only remaining statue from a collection of 21 Gnomes brought to the United Kingdom from Germany by Sir Charles Isham in 1847.

 Garden Gnomes are the smallest of the known Gnome species, at no taller than 1 foot. Forest Gnomes are said to be able to grow to as tall as 3.5 feet. The tallest Gnome on record is Howard the Gnome in Saanich, BC, Canada. Howard stands 28 feet tall!

UNICORNS

NAME: Rufus and Emilia Pentacounial

AGE: Perpetually 13

LOCATION: Black Forest, Germany

HOBBIES: Prancing in fields of flowers, racing rainbows across the sky, poking things with their horns

Unicorns are large, horselike creatures with long, flowing tails and manes. Their most prominent feature is a single sharp, spiraling horn projecting from their foreheads. Often depicted as white horses, Unicorns can exist in any color. Sometimes they are depicted with goatlike beards or feathered hooves. Unicorns are often used in media to symbolize purity, innocence, and light.

STRANDS USED:	2
BACKSTITCH:	DMC 310
AIDA COUNT:	14 (oatmeal)
HOOP SIZE:	7" (18 cm)
FINISHED SIZE:	6" × 6¼" (15 × 16 cm)
FRAMED SIZE:	7" × 7" (18 × 18 cm)

UNICORNS Stitch Pattern

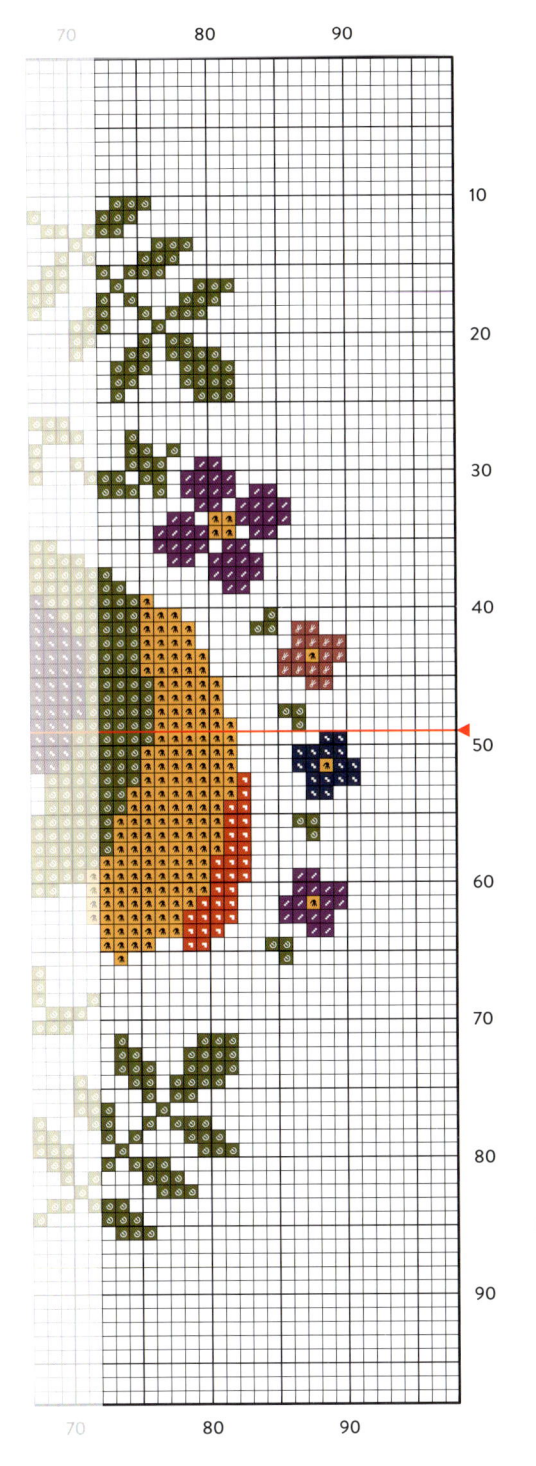

A Unicorn's horn is more properly called an alicorn. Believed to have magic healing properties, alicorn could be purchased in powdered form to add to elixirs and medications.

The Unicorn is the national animal of Scotland. National Unicorn Day in Scotland is April 9.

DMC Floss			
🎤 310	🐾 728	▪️ 312	● Ecru
223	470	552	720

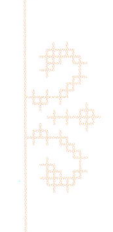

GOBLINS

NAME: Link and Lark

AGE: 12

LOCATION: Taranaki, New Zealand

HOBBIES: Shifting shapes, foraging, specialty mushroom cultivation, general mischief

There are various types of Goblins scattered throughout the world. Most types tend not to maintain a good relationship with humans. Some types may engage in lighthearted mischief toward anyone they encounter, though others are said to be downright hostile or aggressive. Some Goblins are believed to have magical abilities, and most are fairly reclusive. Although goblins come in many shapes, sizes, and colors, most commonly they have greenish skin, long fingernails, pronounced teeth, pointy ears, and large noses. Being mostly nocturnal, almost all Goblins have eyes that are larger than humans' for seeing better in the dark.

STRANDS USED:	2
BACKSTITCH:	DMC 310
AIDA COUNT:	14 (white)
HOOP SIZE:	6" (15 cm)
FINISHED SIZE:	5" × 6" (13 × 15 cm)
FRAMED SIZE:	6" × 8" (15 × 20 cm)

GOBLIN #1 Stitch Pattern

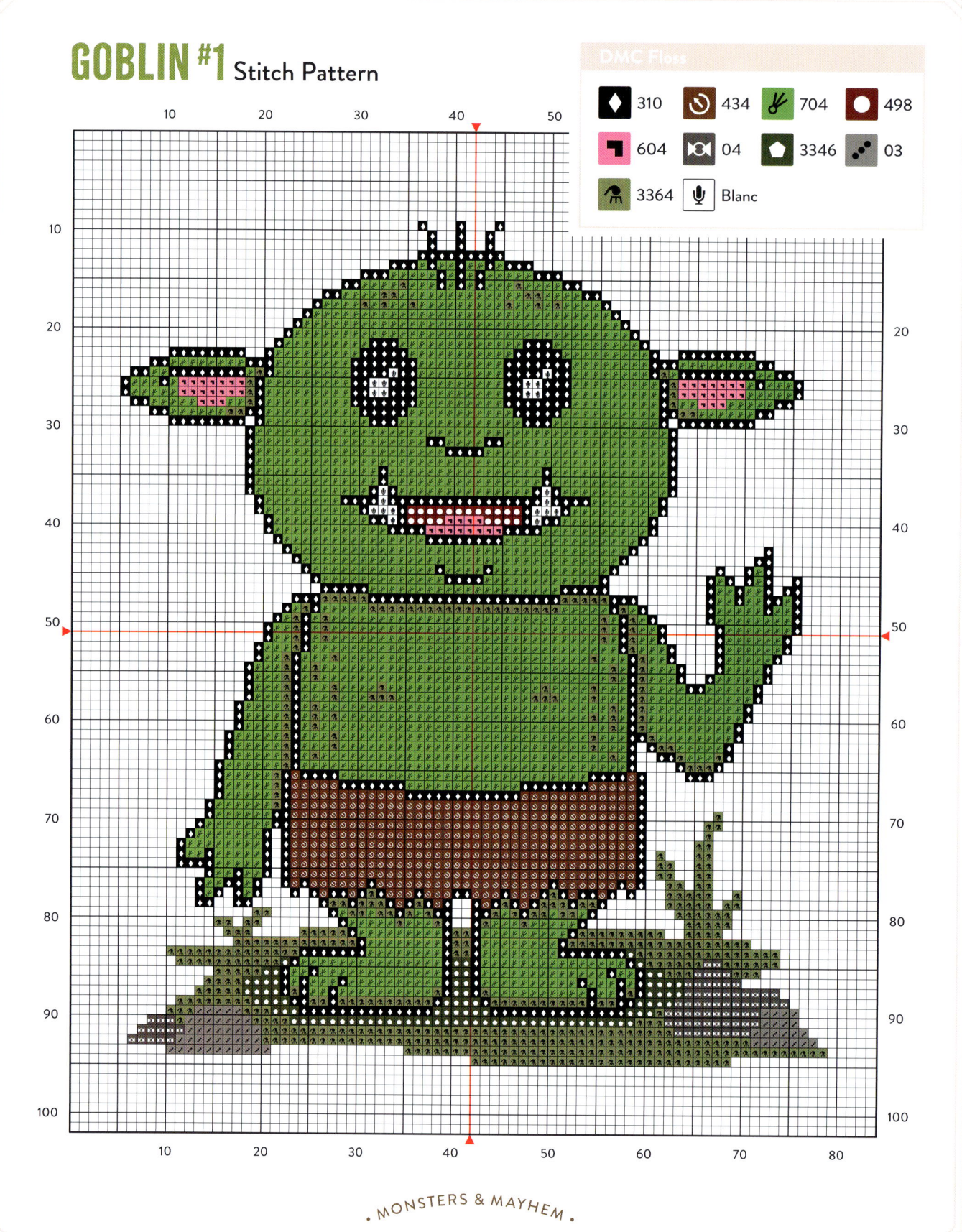

GOBLIN #2 Stitch Pattern

DMC Floss

	310		434		704		666
	604		04		3346		03
	3364		762		Blanc		

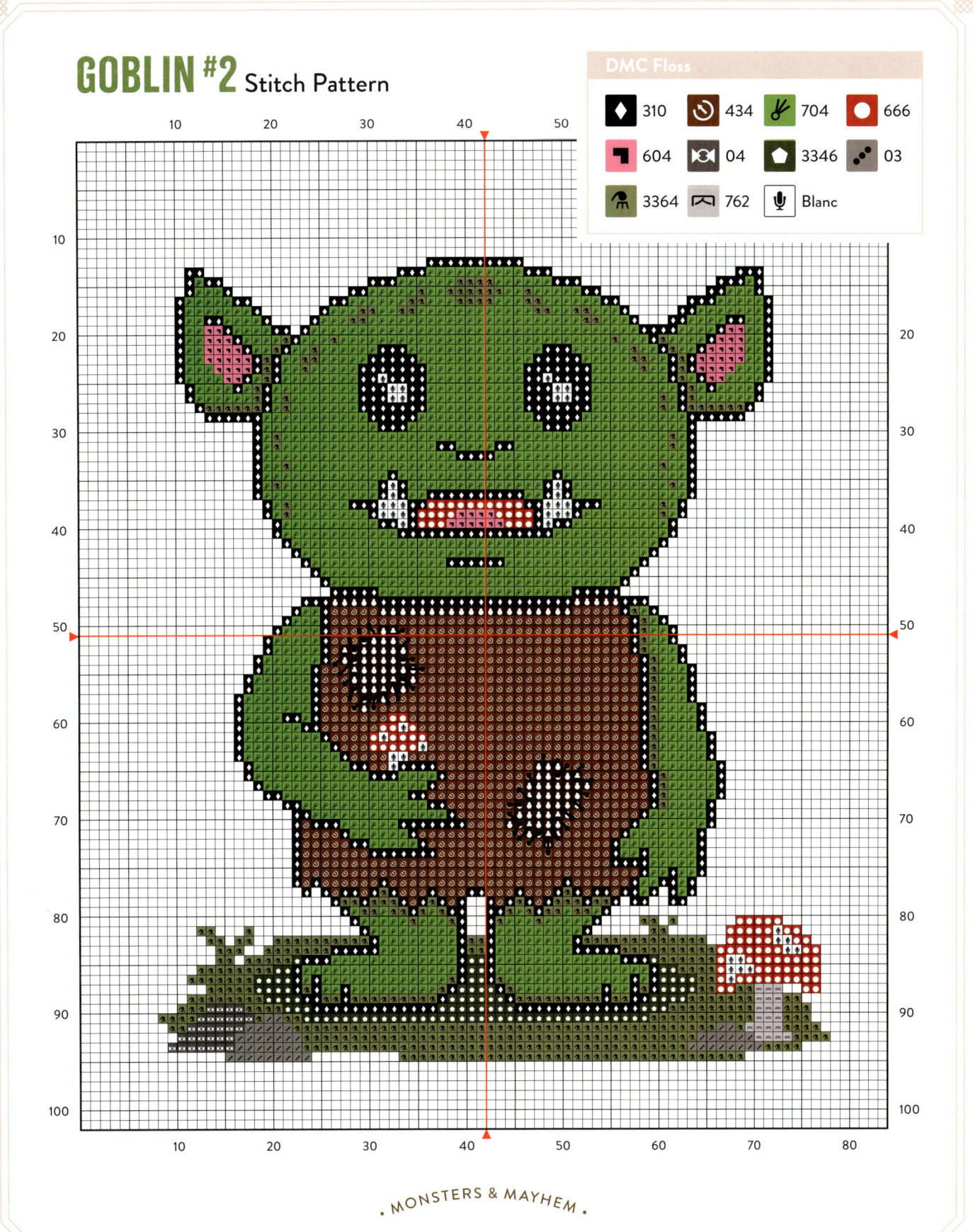

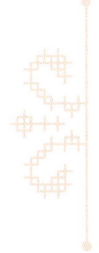
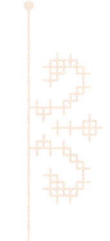

PHOENIX

NAME: Ash

AGE: 499ish

LOCATION: Currently Arabia; born in Heliopolis, Egypt (repeatedly)

HOBBIES: Rising from the ashes of their former life, flying great distances across wide expanses, pottery

The Phoenix in myth is described as being larger than the largest eagle, with bright, almost blinding red-and-gold plumage. The Phoenix is a symbol of rebirth and renewal among many ancient cultures. Most commonly, legend says that every 500 or so years, the Phoenix returns to Heliopolis to build its nest atop the Temple of the Sun. The Phoenix and nest are then engulfed in flames, having been set alight by the sun. The new Phoenix will rise from the ashes of the old and begin its life anew.

STRANDS USED:	2
BACKSTITCH:	DMC 350
AIDA COUNT:	14 (white)
HOOP SIZE:	7" (18 cm)
FINISHED SIZE:	5¾" × 5¾" (14.5 × 14.5 cm)
FRAMED SIZE:	7" × 7" (18 × 18 cm)

PHOENIX Stitch Pattern

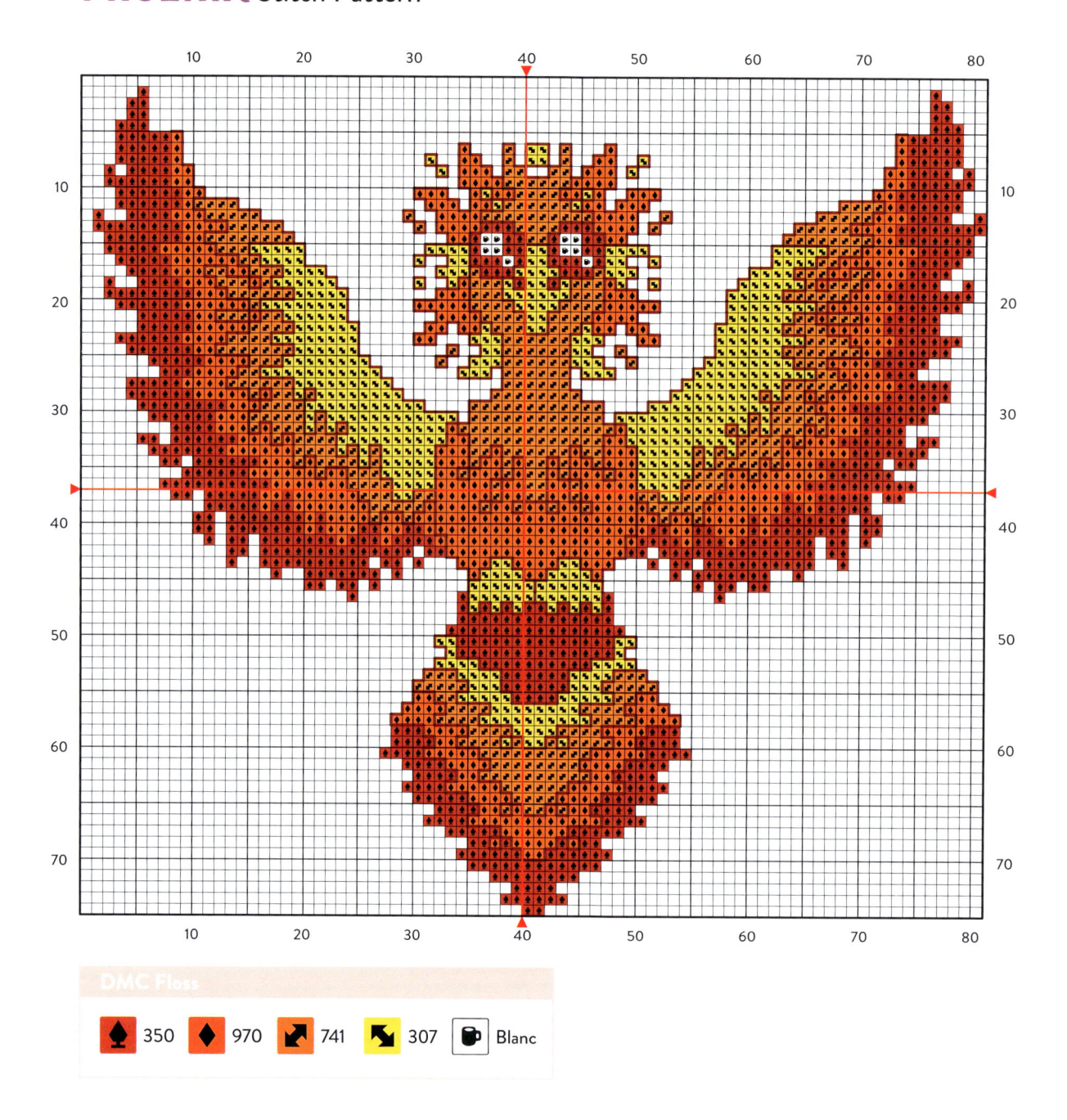

DMC Floss

♠ 350	♦ 970	↗ 741	↘ 307	☕ Blanc

The city of Phoenix, Arizona, was named after the mythical bird and uses it as the official city symbol.

The Phoenix is sometimes depicted with a halo of rays like the sun. This depiction emphasizes the Phoenix's connection with the sun, upon which it relies for its continued rebirth. These rays are similar to those often depicted on Helios, Greek god of the sun. The Phoenix's colors, over time, have also begun to resemble those of the sun and fire, while historically the bird was said to be quite a bit more colorful.

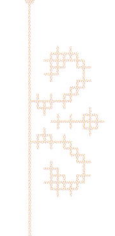

CYCLOPS

NAME: Niton

AGE: Immortal

LOCATION: Serifos, Greece

HOBBIES: A little of everything: building walls, herding sheep, amateur blacksmithing

There are three groups of Cyclops from ancient myth: the three Titan brothers Brontes, Steropes, and Arges, master blacksmiths who forged the most famous weapons of the gods; the cave-dwelling, man-eating goat shepherds bested by Odysseus; and Tiryns and Argos, master wall builders of Mycenae. All are large and powerfully strong and have a single eye in the center of their forehead.

STRANDS USED:	2
BACKSTITCH:	DMC 414
AIDA COUNT:	14 (white)
HOOP SIZE:	7" (18 cm)
FINISHED SIZE:	4" × 6½" (10 × 16.5 cm)
FRAMED SIZE:	5" × 7" (12.5 × 18 cm)

CYCLOPS Stitch Pattern

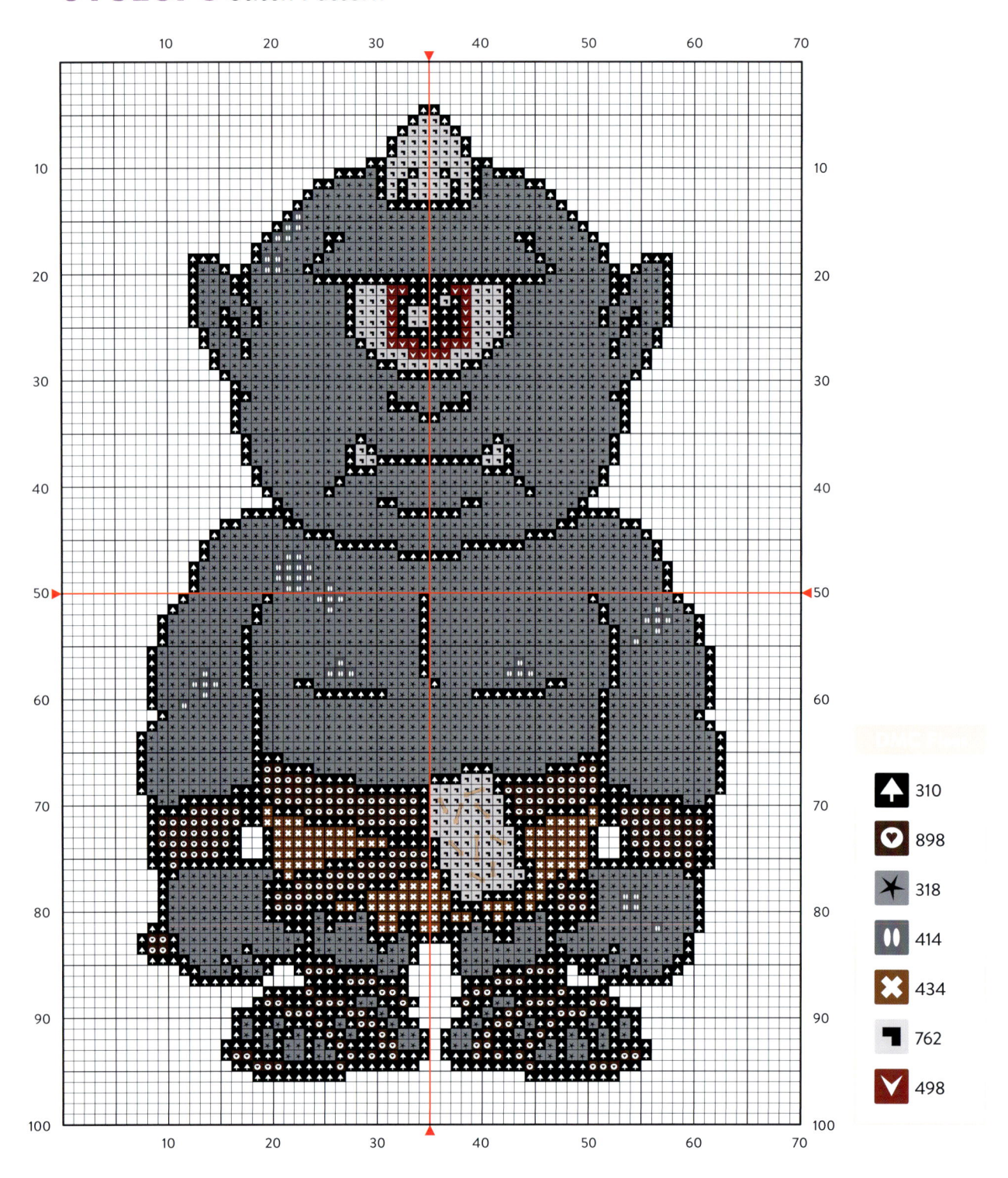

▲	310
♥	898
✶	318
▯▯	414
✕	434
◣	762
▽	498

Odysseus blinded a Cyclops named Polyphemus and later escaped with his men by hanging on to Polyphemus's sheep when they were released to graze.

The Cyclops brothers Brontes, Steropes, and Arges are said to have constructed Zeus's thunderbolt.

The Cyclopean masonry in Mycenae, Greece, is a type of stonework composed of large limestone boulders, assembled sometimes without mortar, and thought to be too large and complex to be built by humans.

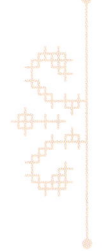

CERBERUS

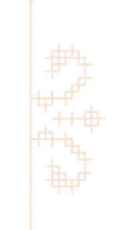

NAME: Liliann, Lily, and Li'l Bear

AGE: Undeterminable in dog years

LOCATION: The Underworld

HOBBIES: Fetch with souls, guarding gates, wrestling, piggyback rides, twirling for biscuits

In Greek mythology, Cerberus is the three-headed dog that was tasked with guarding the gates to the underworld. He belongs to Hades, god of the underworld, and his job is to prevent the dead from escaping. In addition to his three heads, he is sometimes described as having a snakelike tail and serpents growing from his back. Creatures similar to Cerberus are often used in popular culture to protect the entrances to forbidden areas. Our Cerberus was named after Nicole's rescue pooch, Lily, and her three distinct personalities: clingingly anxious and scared of loud noises, aggressively playful, and cuddly-sweet.

STRANDS USED:	2
AIDA COUNT:	14 (white)
HOOP SIZE:	7" (18 cm)
FINISHED SIZE:	6½" × 6¼" (16.5 × 16 cm)
FRAMED SIZE:	7" × 5" (18 × 12.5 cm)

CERBERUS Stitch Pattern

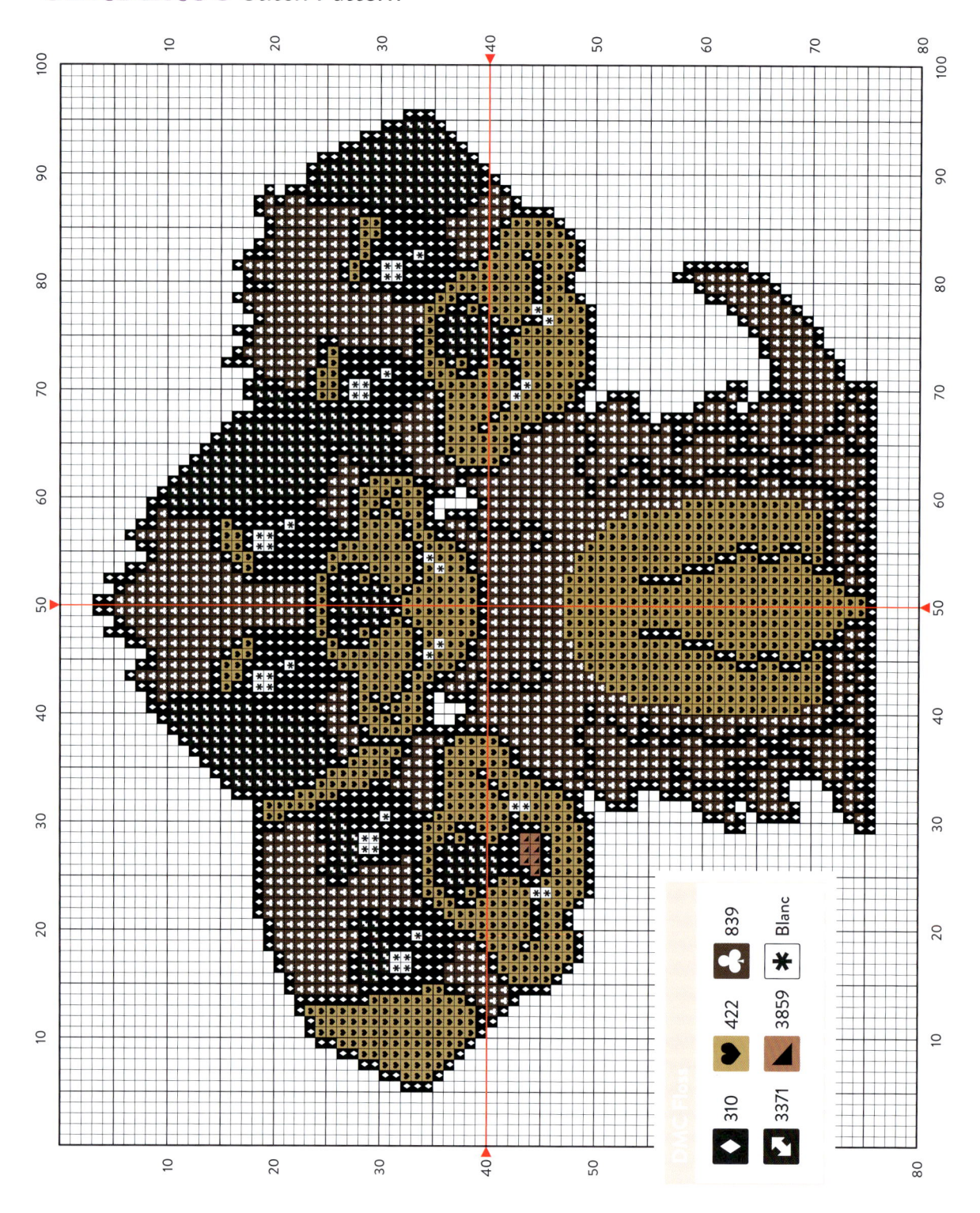

DMC Floss			
◆	310	♣	839
◢	3371	✳	Blanc
♥	422		
◤	3859		

The hero Hercules was given 12 tasks to atone for his crimes and as a show of bravery. His final task was to capture Cerberus and bring him to the land of the living from the underworld—thought to be impossible. Hercules succeeded in his task, however, and then promptly returned Cerberus to his station, guarding the gates.

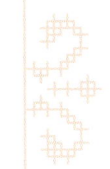

Legendary musician and poet Orpheus also bested Cerberus. He did so by charming the beast with music.

While Cerberus is most often depicted with only three heads, the number of heads in the myths would often vary . . . sometimes it was as many as 50 heads!

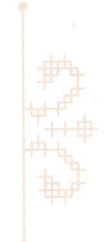

PEGASUS

NAME: Pegasus

AGE: 1,045

LOCATION: Mount Olympus

HOBBIES: Wandering the heavens, soaring among the clouds, assisting in Grand Conquests

Stories of winged horses go back hundreds of thousands of years and span cultures across the globe. But no winged horses will ever be as well known as the Pegasus. Pegasus was a white-winged stallion born of the slain Medusa's blood. He was captured by Bellerophon in order to defeat Chimera, and the two would go on to have many adventures together. Some stories say that after Bellerophon's death, Pegasus came to belong to Athena and was housed in a glorious stable on Mount Olympus.

To create the constellation on your Pegasus, connect the DMC E940 (fun floss named "Glow in the Dark") stitches with a backstitch in the same color.

STRANDS USED:	2
BACKSTITCH:	DMC E940 (Glow)
AIDA COUNT:	14 (navy blue)
HOOP SIZE:	6" (15 cm)
FINISHED SIZE:	9¼" × 7¼" (23.5 × 18.5 cm)
FRAMED SIZE:	10" × 8" (25.5 × 20 cm)

PEGASUS
Stitch Pattern

- 318
- E940 (glow)
- 793
- 158
- 29
- 3799
- 312

- C318
- C820
- C823
- Blanc

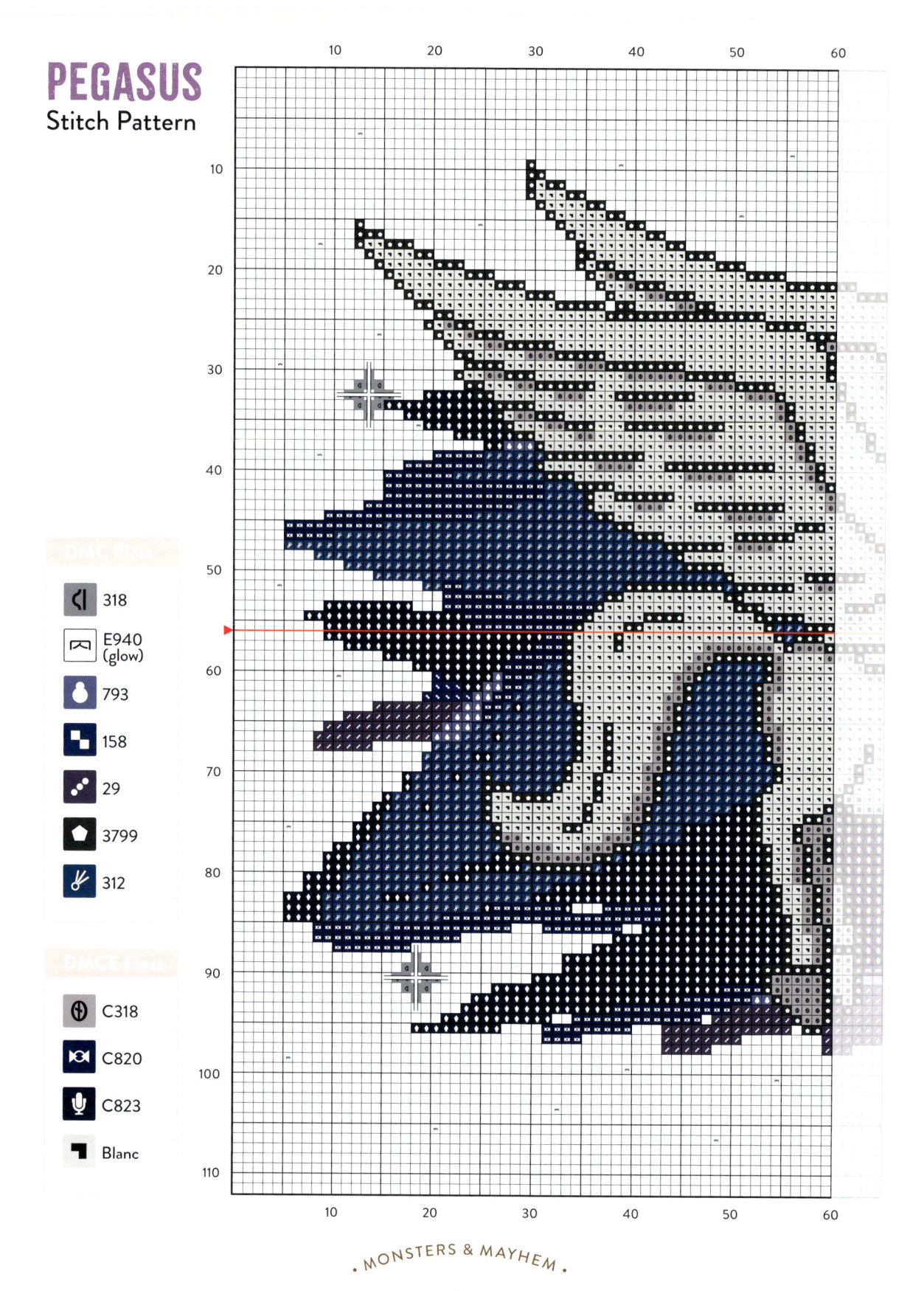

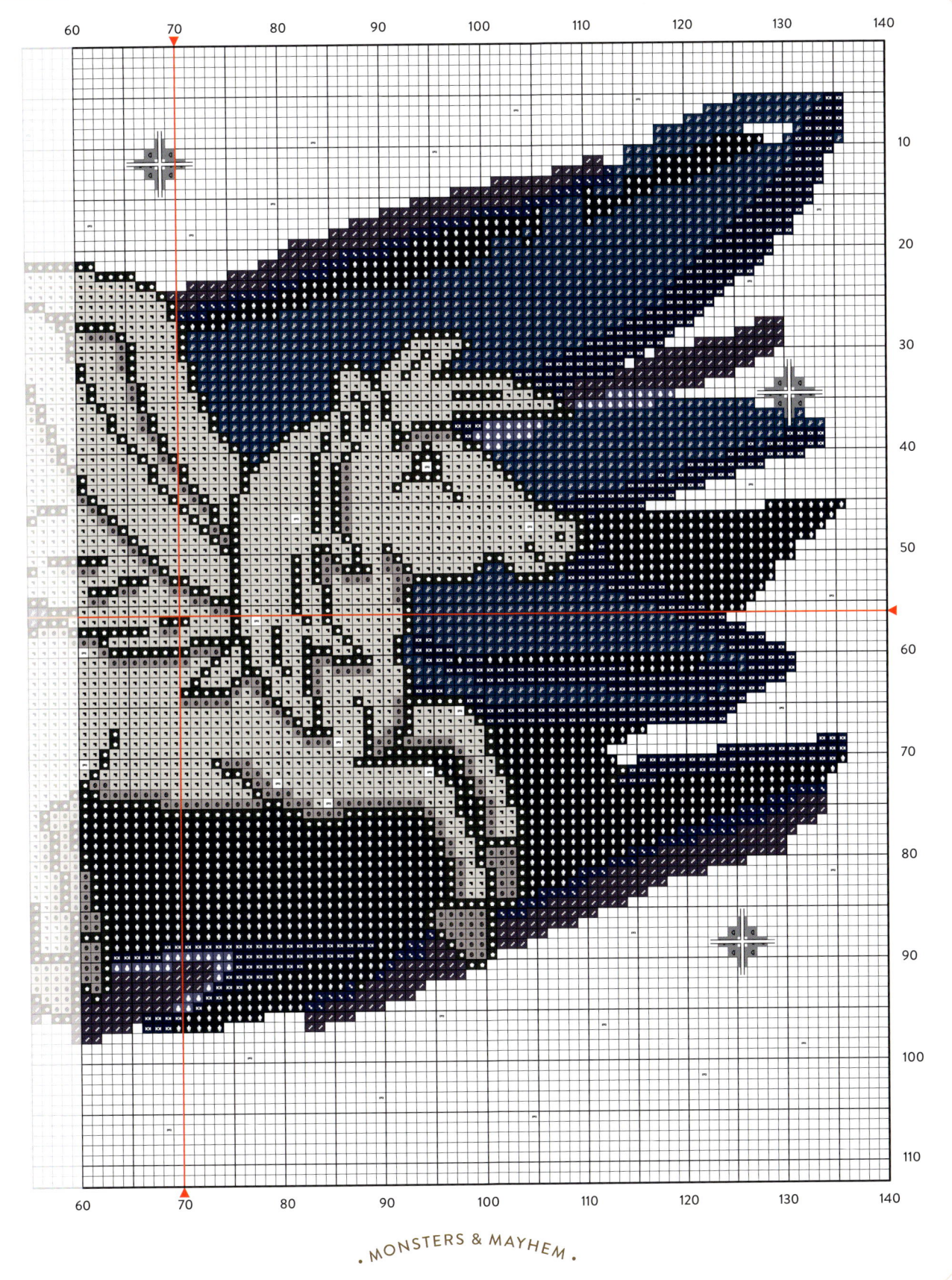

PEGASUS Stitch Pattern, *continued*

Pegasus Constellation

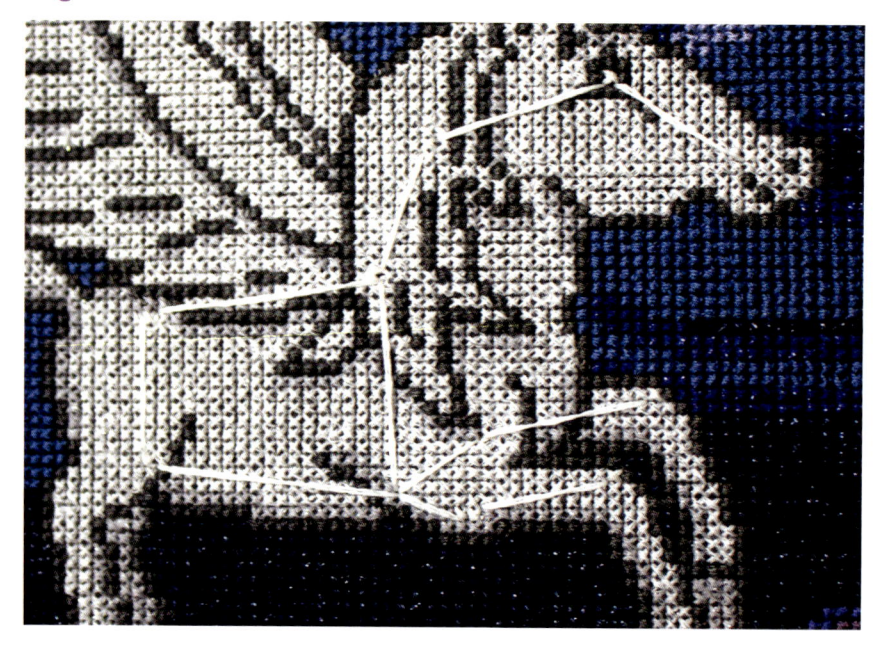

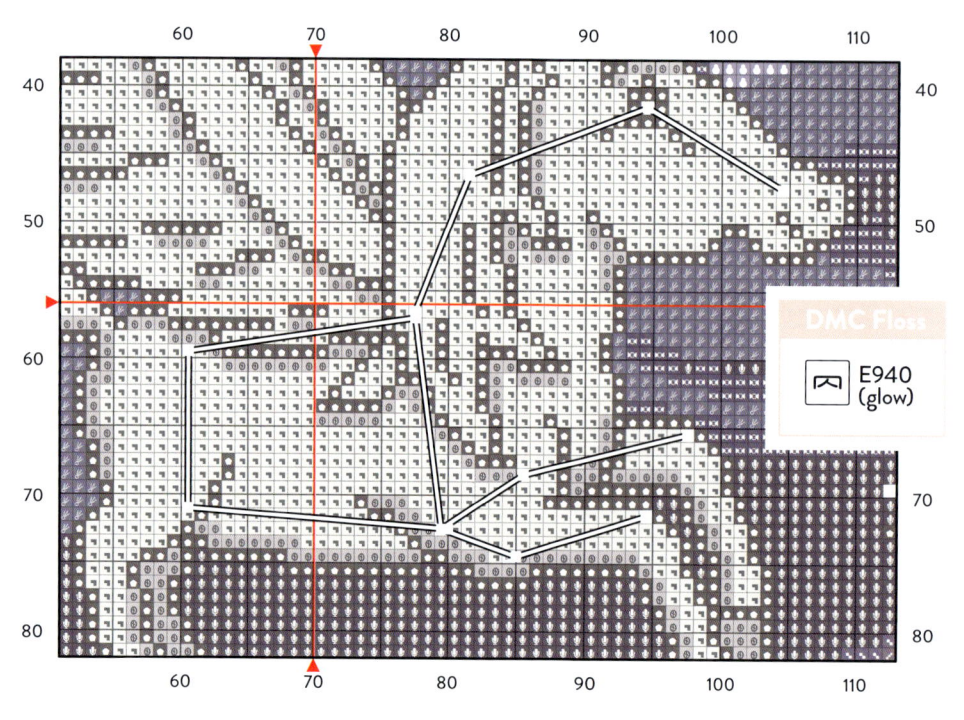

DMC Floss

	E940 (glow)

Feel free to skip the connecting backstitch if you'd like the constellation to show simply the star points, or stitch the glow stitches in DMC Blanc to remove the constellation completely.

Dark fabric can be difficult to work with. Try using a lamp behind your cloth, sitting in sunlight, or placing a sheet of white paper on your lap below your stitching to better see the holes in the fabric.

Of the 88 constellations, the Pegasus constellation is the seventh largest. It's composed of 17 main stars (ours here has only 11), the brightest of which is called *Epsilon Pegasi*, also known as Enif.

Pegasus often carried the thunderbolts for Zeus.

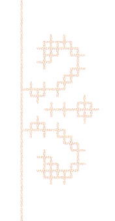

Myth says that Pegasus had power over water and that he could create a magical spring of water with just his hoof. It is said he also created Hippocrene, a famous spring located on Mount Helicon in Boeotia, Greece.

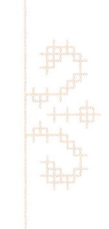

MINOTAUR

NAME: Asterion

AGE: 43

LOCATION: Crete, Greece

HOBBIES: Puzzles, playing tag with Athenians, playing hide-and-seek with Athenians, BBQ

The Minotaur is the doomed offspring of Pasiphae and a snow-white bull. Pasiphae was cursed to fall in love with the bull as a punishment for her husband Minos's refusal to sacrifice that bull to honor Poseidon. With no cage strong enough to hold the vicious creature, the Minotaur was trapped within the Labyrinth. Described as half man, half bull, the Minotaur is most commonly depicted as having the body of a man and the head and tail of a bull. The pattern making the frame around our Minotaur is called meander, also known as Greek key. We felt this ancient pattern was reminiscent of a labyrinth for our Minotaur to be trapped within.

STRANDS USED:	2
BACKSTITCH:	DMC 310
AIDA COUNT:	14 (white)
HOOP SIZE:	7" (18 cm)
FINISHED SIZE:	5" × 6½" (12.5 × 16.5 cm)
FRAMED SIZE:	5" × 7" (12.5 × 18 cm)

MINOTAUR Stitch Pattern

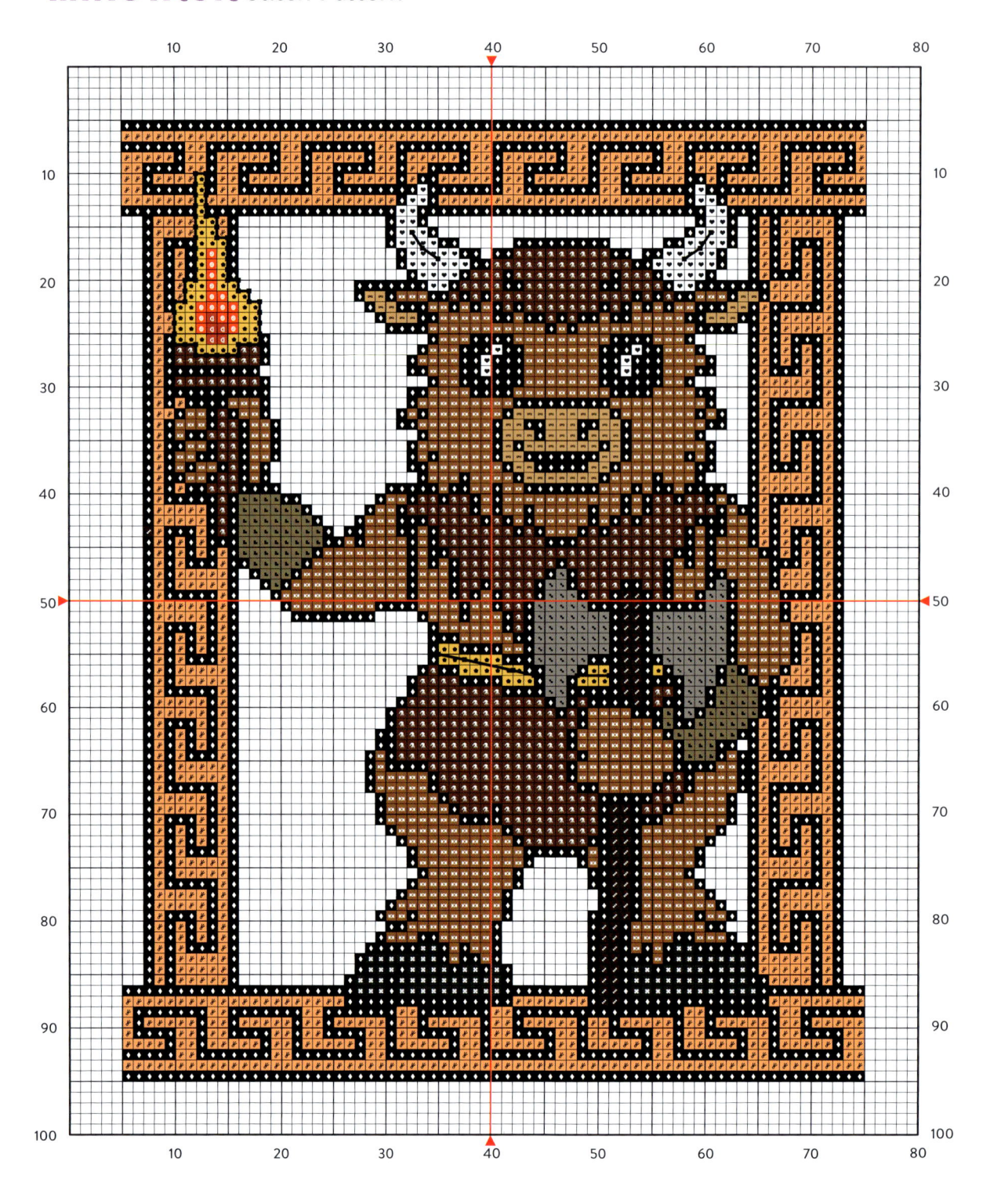

The Minotaur appears briefly in Dante's Inferno, having been damned for his violent nature.

Aegus, the king of Athens, in order to avoid a plague as punishment for killing Androgeus, was compelled to sacrifice young men and women to the Minotaur. A hero named Theseus, with the help of Androgeus's sister, then slayed the Minotaur and rescued the young Athenians.

DMC Floss

◆ 310	⬛ 435	◼ 03	⬤ 946	⬠ 444	◼ 642	▱ 437	
⚡ 3825	⬛ 433	⬤ 938	◀ 900	♥ Blanc	❈ 3799		

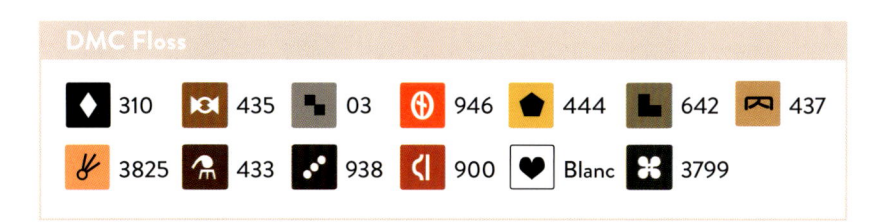

MOTHMAN

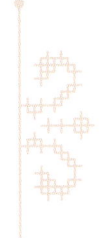

NAME: David

AGE: 50

LOCATION: West Virginia, USA

HOBBIES: Sleeping in backyards, chasing cars,
predicting the future

Exclusive to Point Pleasant, West Virginia, and the surrounding areas, the Mothman is reported as a cross between a large owl-like creature and a slender yet muscular man. It is said to have large, hypnotic, glowing red eyes and a 10-foot wingspan. Some people believe the Mothman is an omen of oncoming disasters. Reports of its appearance increase in the days leading up to a disaster and seem to disappear in the aftermath. Mothman is usually depicted as creepy and scary. We wanted our Mothman to be more sympathetic. Maybe he's not out tonight for evil, just a little general lurking, and didn't mean to startle anyone.

STRANDS USED:	2
AIDA COUNT:	14 (white)
HOOP SIZE:	6" (15 cm)
FINISHED SIZE:	5½" × 4⅜" (14 × 11 cm)
FRAMED SIZE:	7" × 5" (18 × 12.5 cm)

MOTHMAN Stitch Pattern

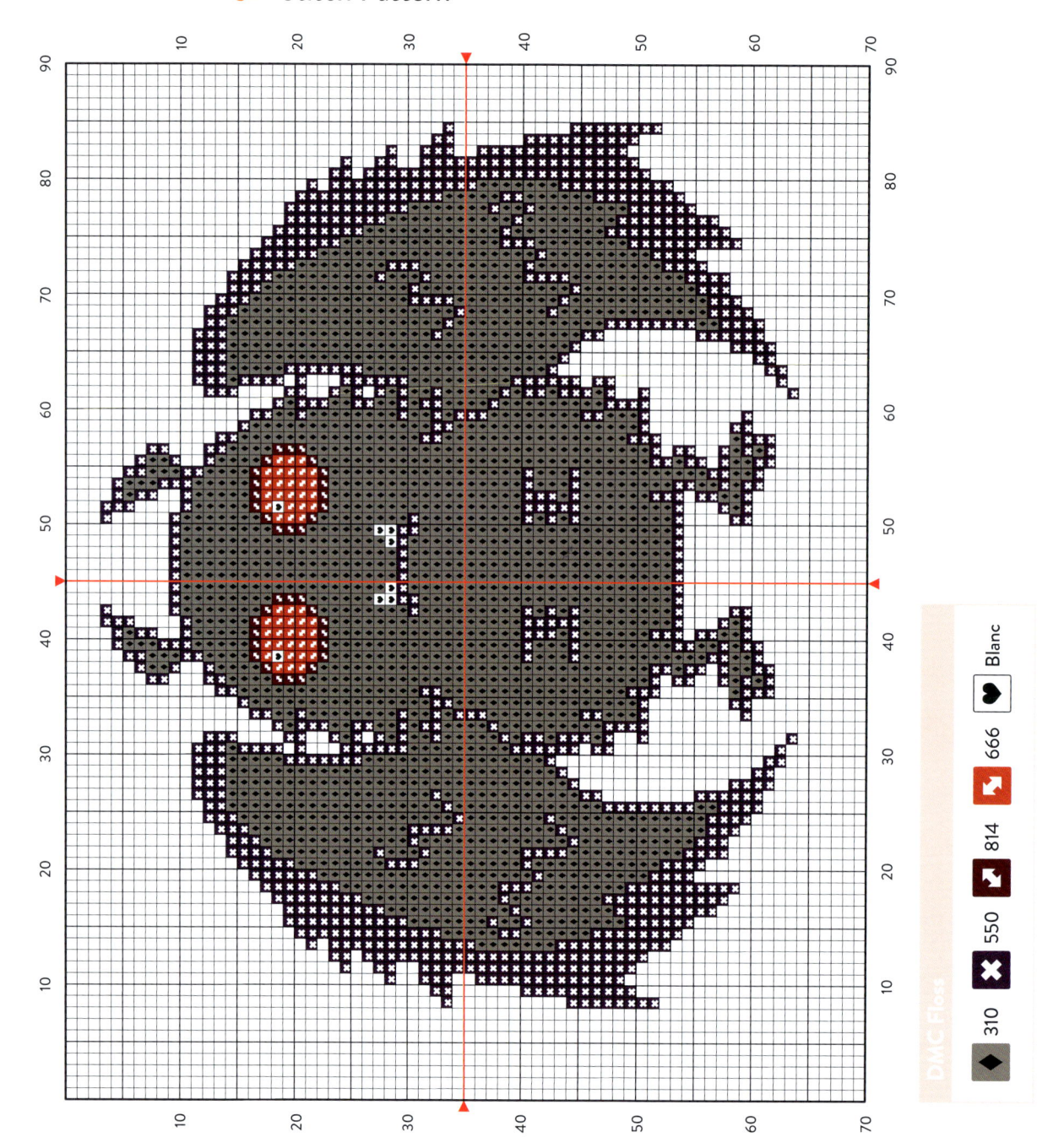

DMC Floss		
310	✖	550
◆		
814	◥	666
◥		
Blanc	♥	

Every fall, Point Pleasant, West Virginia, holds a festival in celebration of the Mothman, complete with food, music, and guest speakers. Point Pleasant is also home to the world's only Mothman Museum, as well as an amazing 12-foot-tall, polished-steel Mothman statue.

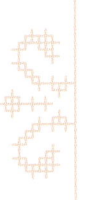 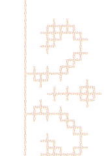

The Mothman has recently been seen around the Chicago, Illinois, area.

The Mothman's eyes are almost always the first thing people notice during an encounter.

BIGFOOT

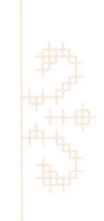

NAME: Footsy

AGE: 34

LOCATION: Assorted woods, North America

HOBBIES: Throwing stones, singing,
long walks in the woods

Sightings of humanoid apelike creatures have been reported all over the world. Bigfoot, or Sasquatch, is a large, hairy creature most commonly reported in North America. While Bigfoot himself is most often associated with the Pacific Northwest, other similar creatures, such as the Honey Island Swamp Monster, Skunk Apes, and Fouke Monster, have been reported throughout the US. Worldwide, relatives of the Bigfoot may include the Yeren, Mapinguari, Yowi, and, of course, Yeti.

STRANDS USED:	2
AIDA COUNT:	14 (white)
HOOP SIZE:	6" (15 cm)
FINISHED SIZE:	10" × 7¼" (25.5 × 18.5 cm)
FRAMED SIZE:	10" × 8" (25.5 × 20 cm)

BIGFOOT
Stitch Pattern

DMC Floss

✪	702
🌲	700
✖	437
▽	703
✳	3761
◉	434
⬆	986
▼	02
✿	648
☾	Blanc
🎤	666
✺	762
♇	744
↻	743
▓	498
⦂	938
◩	422
◆	310

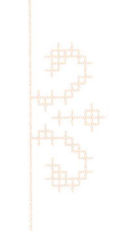

YETI

NAME: Yolanda

AGE: 32

LOCATION: Himalayan mountains

HOBBIES: Pretending to be a polar bear, making snow yetis, ice sculpting

Believed to be a species relative to the Bigfoot, the Yeti, or Abominable Snowman, is typically only seen in the Himalayan mountains of Asia. Yetis share many similar characteristics with the Bigfoot. Although usually depicted as having bright-snow-white fur, Yetis have been reported to occasionally have black, gray, or light-brown fur. They can also range in size from approximately 15 feet tall to only about 3 feet tall, depending on the variety of Yeti encountered. Our Yeti is stitched on light-blue Aida as background sky. For a nighttime alternative, stitch her on navy Aida and leave off the clouds.

STRANDS USED:	2
AIDA COUNT:	14 (light blue)
HOOP SIZE:	6" (15 cm)
FINISHED SIZE:	10" × 7½" (25.5 × 19 cm)
FRAMED SIZE:	10" × 8" (25.5 × 20 cm)

YETI
Stitch Pattern

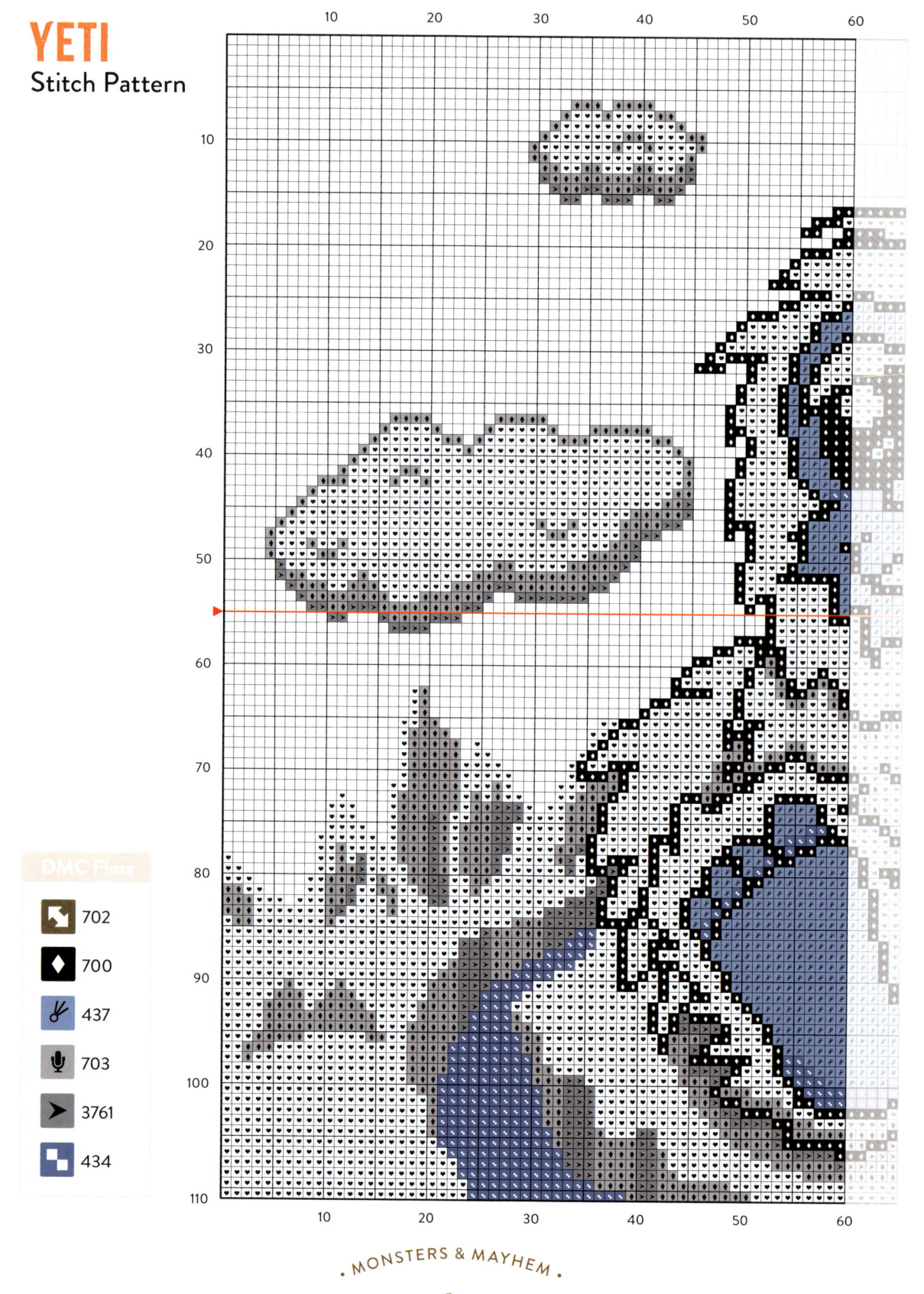

DMC Floss

- 702
- 700
- 437
- 703
- 3761
- 434

. MONSTERS & MAYHEM .

62

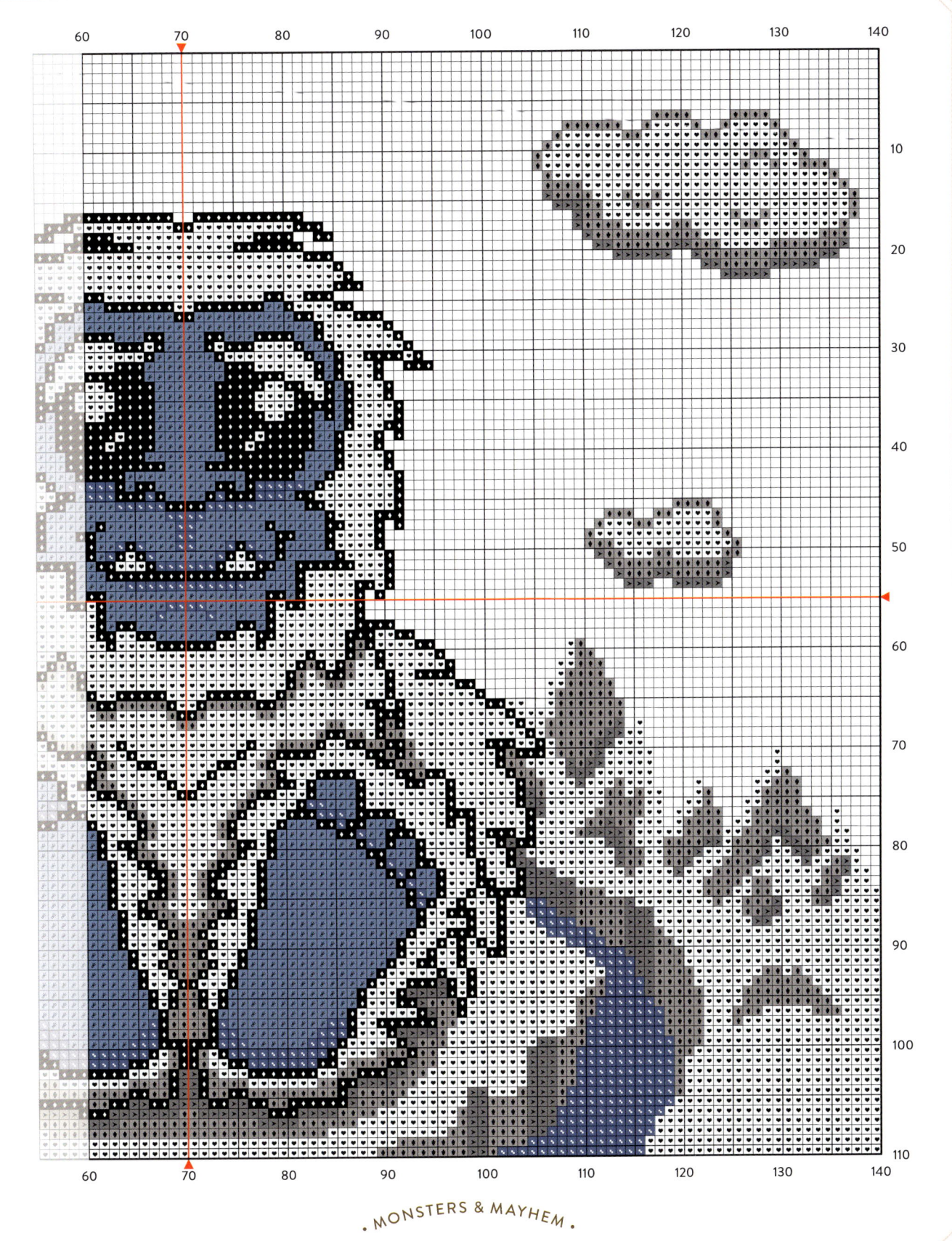

JACKALOPE

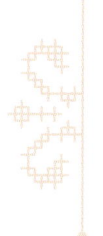
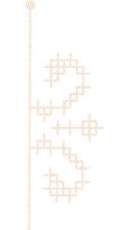

NAME: Bean

AGE: 15

LOCATION: American West

HOBBIES: Mimicking human voices; sipping whiskey;
running super, super fast

Originally believed to be found only in Wyoming, Jackalopes have more recently been spotted in states throughout the American West and in parts of Mexico. Jackalopes are said to resemble a jackrabbit with antelope horns. They have beautiful singing voices but can be very aggressive and territorial.

STRANDS USED:	2
BACKSTITCH:	DMC 310
AIDA COUNT:	14 (white)
HOOP SIZE:	6" (15 cm)
FINISHED SIZE:	5" × 6⅜" (12.5 × 16 cm)
FRAMED SIZE:	6" × 8" (15 × 20 cm)

JACKALOPE Stitch Pattern

Jackalope taxidermy is very popular. The mounts are created by attaching deer antlers to a taxidermy jackrabbit pelt. This kind of taxidermy, the combining of two or more animals to create something unique, is called a gaff. One famous example of gaff taxidermy is P. T. Barnum's Fiji Mermaid, made by sewing the front half of a monkey to the back half of a fish.

Jackalopes are considered so dangerous that frontier hunters were once advised to wear metal stovepipes on their legs to guard against being gored.

While it failed to become the Official Mythological Creature of the state of Wyoming, the Jackalope did become the mascot of the Wyoming Lottery.

DMC Floss

640	3021	310	Blanc	3023	3024
433	223	437	3790	435	436
470	744	743	730	733	

LAKE MONSTER

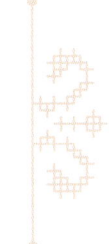

NAME: Loci

AGE: Unknown

LOCATION: Loch Ness in the Scottish Highlands

HOBBIES: Sonar hide and seek, pretending to be logs, peeking at tourists

The most famous lake monster in world is the one that resides in Scotland's Loch Ness. There have been, however, sightings of similar large aquatic animals in lakes and rivers all over the world. Some people believe these animals are descendants of ancient plesiosaurs that somehow escaped extinction.

STRANDS USED:	2
BACKSTITCH:	DMC Blanc
AIDA COUNT:	14 (navy blue)
HOOP SIZE:	7" (18 cm)
FINISHED SIZE:	5½" × 4" (14 × 10 cm)
FRAMED SIZE:	7" × 5" (18 × 12.5 cm)

LAKE MONSTER Stitch Pattern

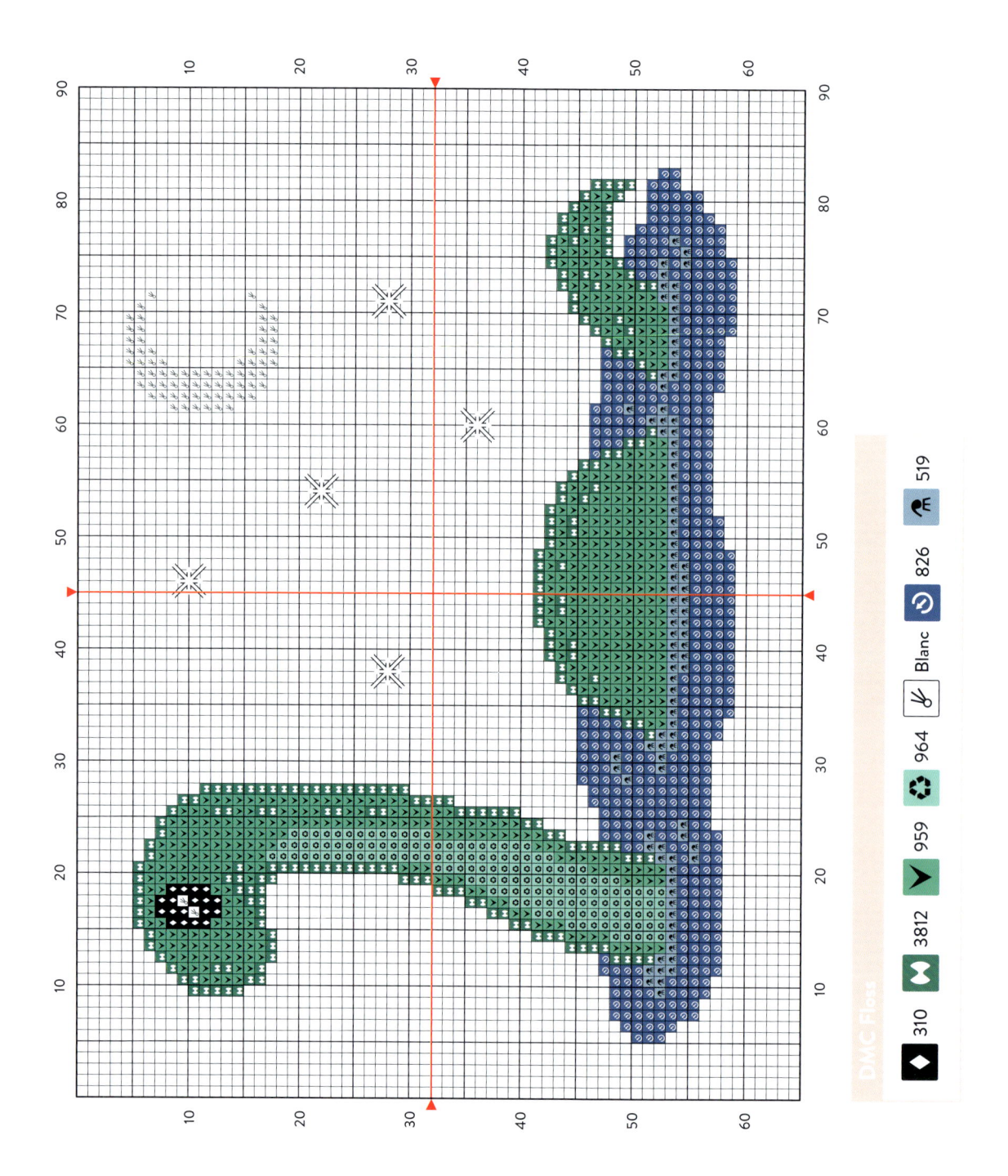

Dark fabric can be difficult to work with. Try using a lamp behind your cloth, sitting in sunlight, or placing a sheet of white paper on your lap below your stitching to better see the holes in the fabric.

Your Lake Monster can also be stitched on light-blue Aida without the sky elements for a daytime scene. Or if you're brave, stitch the moon and stars with DMC E940 "Glow in the Dark."

The second-most-famous Lake Monster is Champ, or Champy, of Lake Champlain in northern New York and Vermont. Champy has been sighted in both US states.

The US state of Georgia has a river monster named the Altamaha-ha. The possible scientific relationship between river- and lake-based monsters is still unresolved.

MERPEOPLE

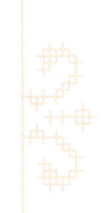

AGE: Various

LOCATION: Deep seas worldwide

HOBBIES: Singing, bead making, storytelling, seaweed basket weaving

Merpeople or Merfolk are mythological beings with the upper body of a human attached to the tail of a fish. Mermaids are much more commonly spotted than Mermen. While generally believed to be mostly benevolent, they are known to cause storms, shipwrecks, or floods if wronged or insulted. Our Merpeople include a variety of skin, hair, and fin colors. Feel free to mix and match to make your Merpeople however you'd like. Why not try swapping out their background elements too?

STRANDS USED:	2
AIDA COUNT:	14 (white)
HOOP SIZE:	3" (7.5 cm)
FINISHED SIZE:	2⅜" × 2⅜" (6 × 6 cm)
FRAMED SIZE:	3" × 3" (7.5 × 7.5 cm)

MERPEOPLE Stitch Patterns

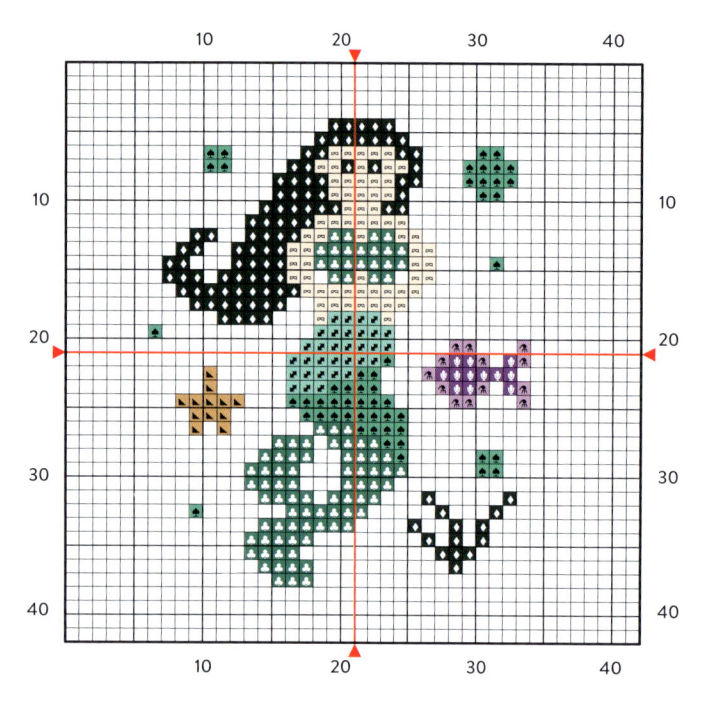

Merpeople #1

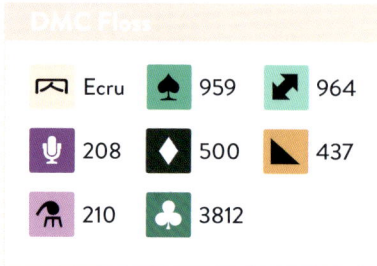

Ecru		959		964	
208		500		437	
210		3812			

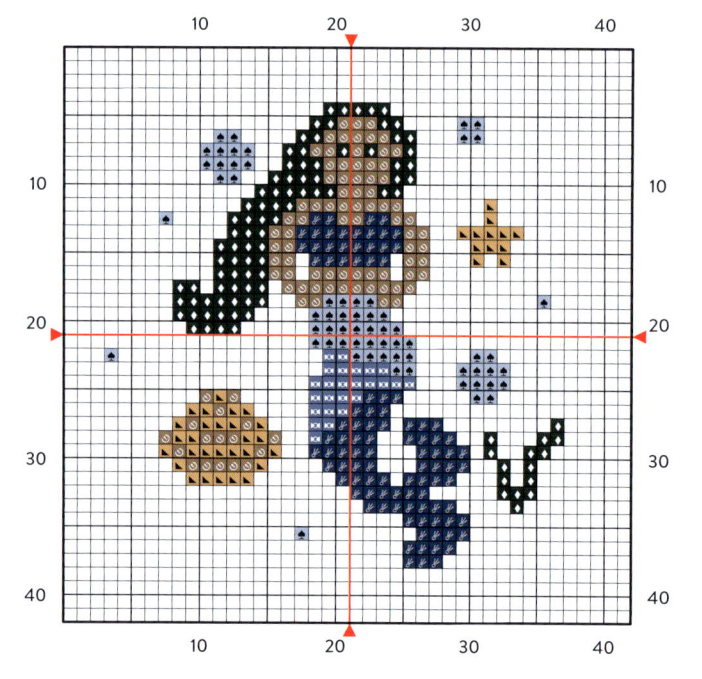

Merpeople #2

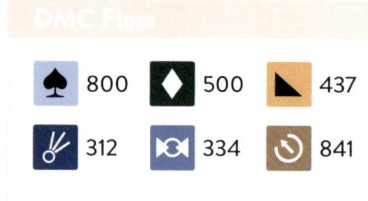

800		500		437	
312		334		841	

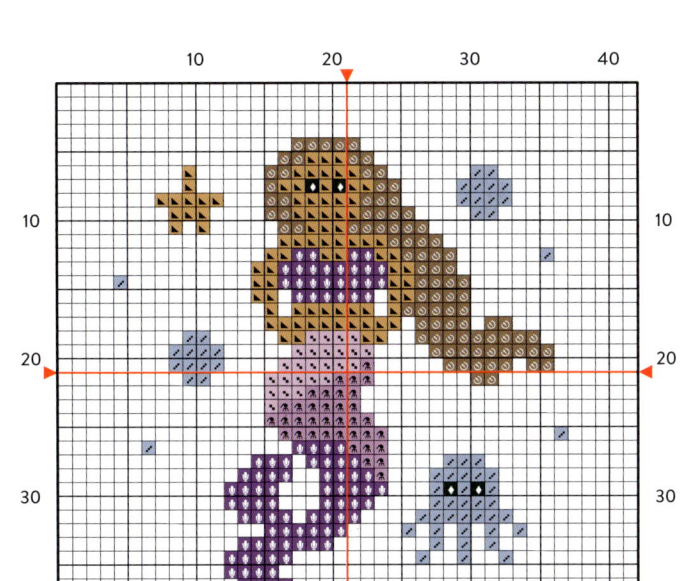
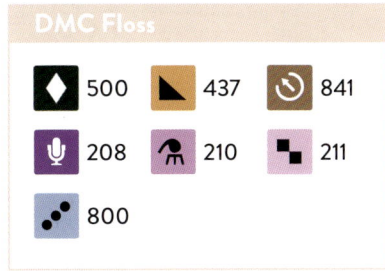

Merpeople #3

DMC Floss		
◆ 500	◣ 437	↻ 841
⚲ 208	🐾 210	◼ 211
⦙ 800		

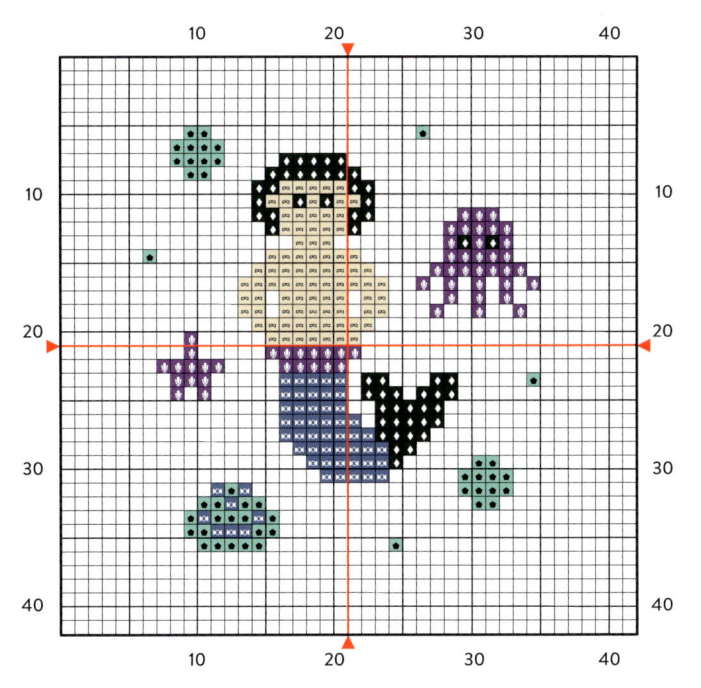
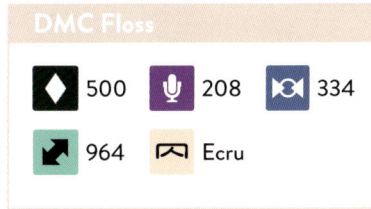

Merpeople #4

DMC Floss		
◆ 500	⚲ 208	⋈ 334
◤ 964	⌒ Ecru	

MERPEOPLE Stitch Patterns, *continued*

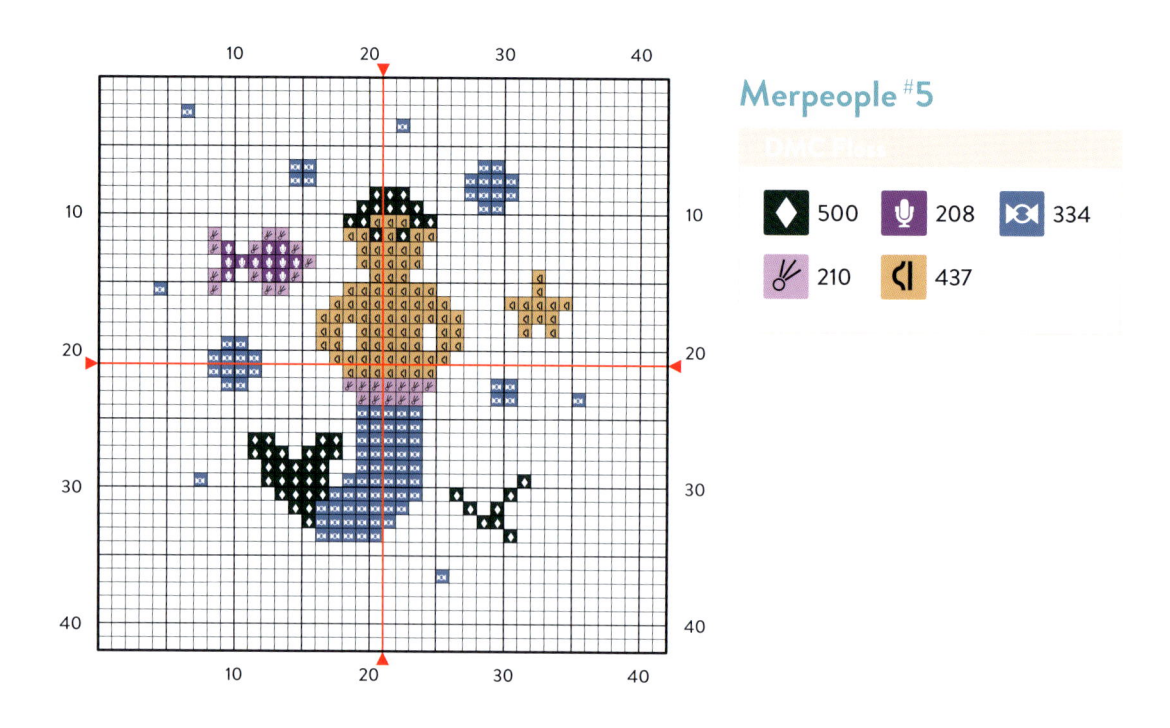

Merpeople #5

DMC Floss

- ◆ 500
- 🎤 208
- ⋈ 334
- 🖌 210
- ◁ 437

Merpeople should not be confused with Sirens. Sirens, who often lure men to shipwreck and death with their enchanted singing, are described as having large bird-like wings. Whether or not Sirens have fishlike tails or clawed feet is up for debate.

One can capture and keep a Merperson by stealing something of theirs with great sentimental value. As long as the item is kept hidden, the Merperson will stay. If they find the item, they will return at once to the sea.

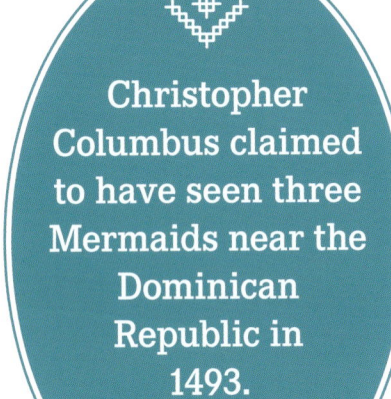

Christopher Columbus claimed to have seen three Mermaids near the Dominican Republic in 1493.

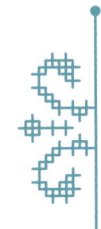 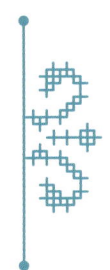

According to author Hans Christian Andersen, Merpeople can sometimes live up to 300 years. When a Merperson's life does come to an end, their body slowly dissolves and becomes foam on the surface of the ocean.

Some people believe that ancient reports of mermaid sightings were actually a result of sailors who, delirious from long voyages, spotted manatees from a great distance and thought them to be women.

KRAKEN

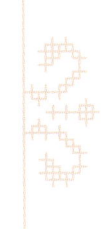

NAME: Hans Storthavsuge

AGE: Unknown

LOCATION: Norwegian Sea

HOBBIES: Fishing, collecting boats, knitting

Said to live in the sea between Norway and Iceland, the Kraken is an enormous sea creature commonly described as a resembling an octopus or other cephalopod. The Kraken is known to be ferocious and to attack ships with its giant tentacles, crushing them or pulling them down into the sea. While our pattern calls for light-blue fabric, Kraken would look great on any light-colored fabric, including white. If you want to try stitching him on navy blue or black, stitch the boat in DMC 436 Tan instead of DMC 310 Black.

STRANDS USED:	2
BACKSTITCH:	DMC 310
AIDA COUNT:	14 (light blue)
HOOP SIZE:	4" (10 cm)
FINISHED SIZE:	3½" × 3⅜" (9 × 8.5 cm)
FRAMED SIZE:	4" × 4" (10 × 10 cm)

KRAKEN Stitch Pattern

While the creature in Jules Verne's Twenty Thousand Leagues Under the Sea *more closely resembles a giant squid, the book is credited with making the Kraken myth famous.*

The Kraken is usually described as being similar to an octopus, but it is believed to have been inspired by the giant squid.

The earliest accounts of the Kraken describe it as more crab-like than squid or octopus.

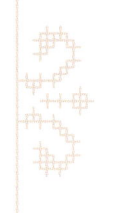

DRAGON

NAME: Dara

AGE: 1,012

LOCATION: Wherever, mostly western Europe

HOBBIES: Flying, breathing fire,
munching on villagers

While there are many types of Dragons appearing in folklore worldwide, one of the most recognizable is the European or Western Dragon. These dragons are large, lizard-like creatures with long necks, and they sport sharp teeth. They have enormous leathery wings capable of carrying them high into the sky. These Dragons are usually depicted with a set of wings and with either four limbs or two limbs. They breathe fire and are often described as protecting gold or other riches.

STRANDS USED:	2
AIDA COUNT:	14 (white)
HOOP SIZE:	6" (15 cm)
FINISHED SIZE:	9¼" × 4¾" (23.5 × 12 cm)
FRAMED SIZE:	10" × 8" (25.5 × 20 cm)

DRAGON Stitch Pattern

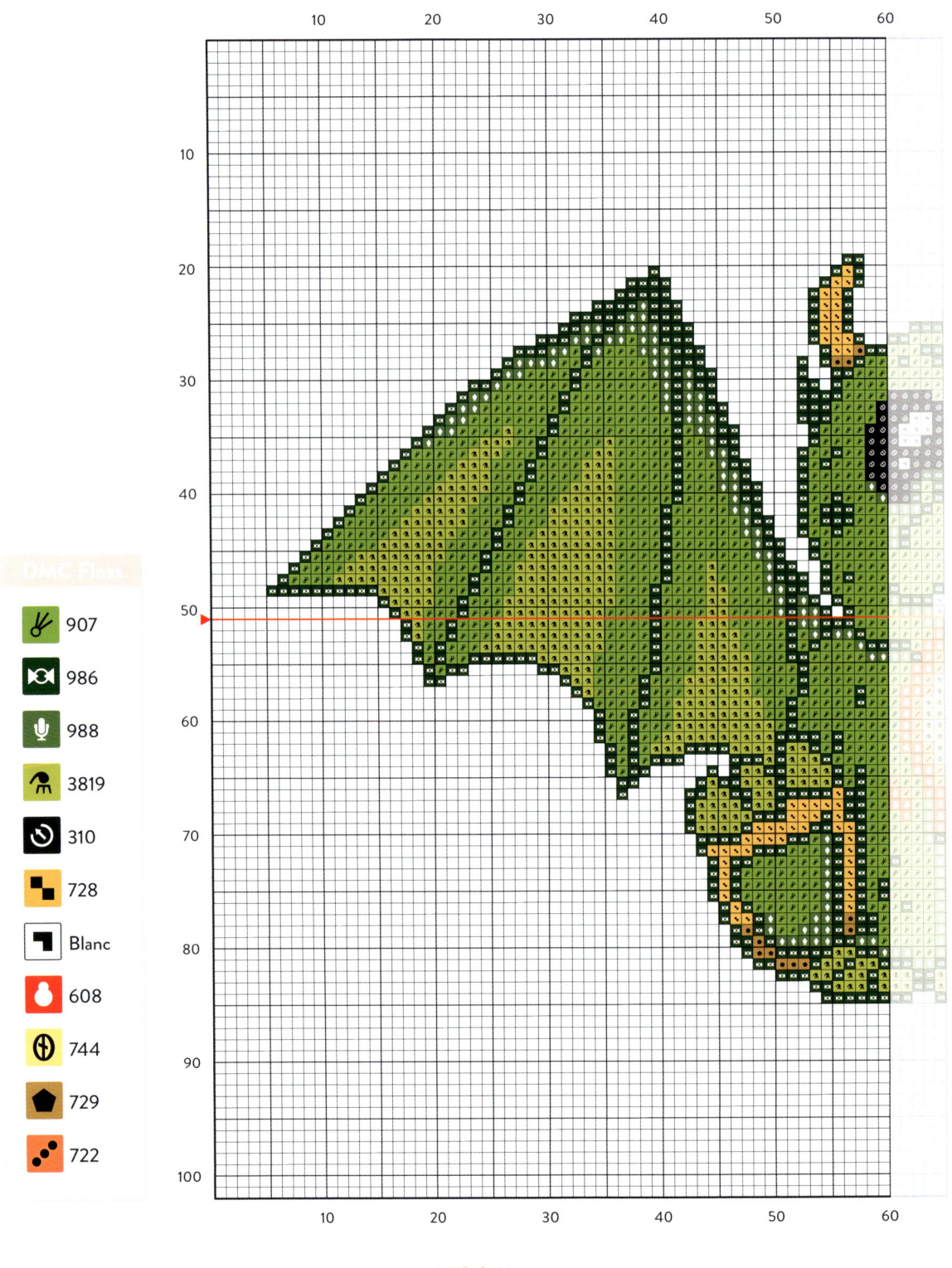

DMC Floss

⚡	907
✇	986
⬇	988
⚘	3819
◑	310
◼	728
◣	Blanc
♟	608
⊕	744
⬟	729
⋰	722

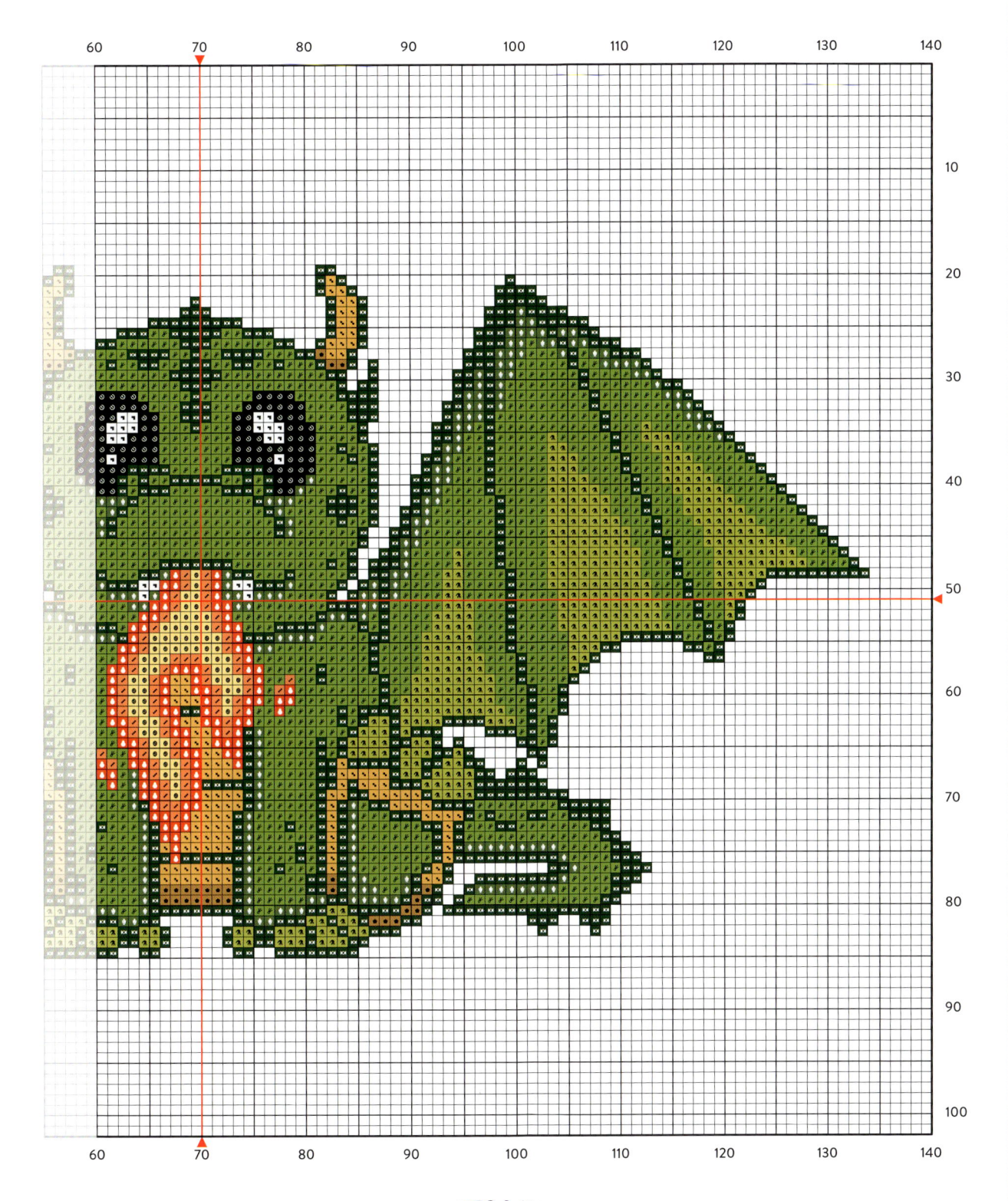

GARGOYLE

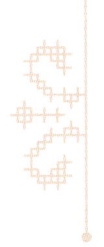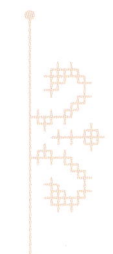

NAME: Sir Maximus Nicolodius

AGE: Immortal

LOCATION: New Orleans, Louisiana, USA

HOBBIES: Lurking, looming,
scaring away Evil Spirits, pickleball

Gargoyle sculptures were originally used as architectural elements for diverting water away from the sides of buildings, thus reducing erosion. They were sculpted as fantastic animals, creepy humans, and bizarre creatures to, as legend says, serve a second purpose of protecting the building from evil spirits. In more recent times, Gargoyles make appearances in everything from cartoons to movies to tabletop games.

STRANDS USED:	2
AIDA COUNT:	14 (white)
HOOP SIZE:	6" (15 cm)
FINISHED SIZE:	10" × 11⅝" (25.5 × 29.5 cm)
FRAMED SIZE:	11" × 14" (28 × 35.5 cm)

GARGOYLE Stitch Pattern

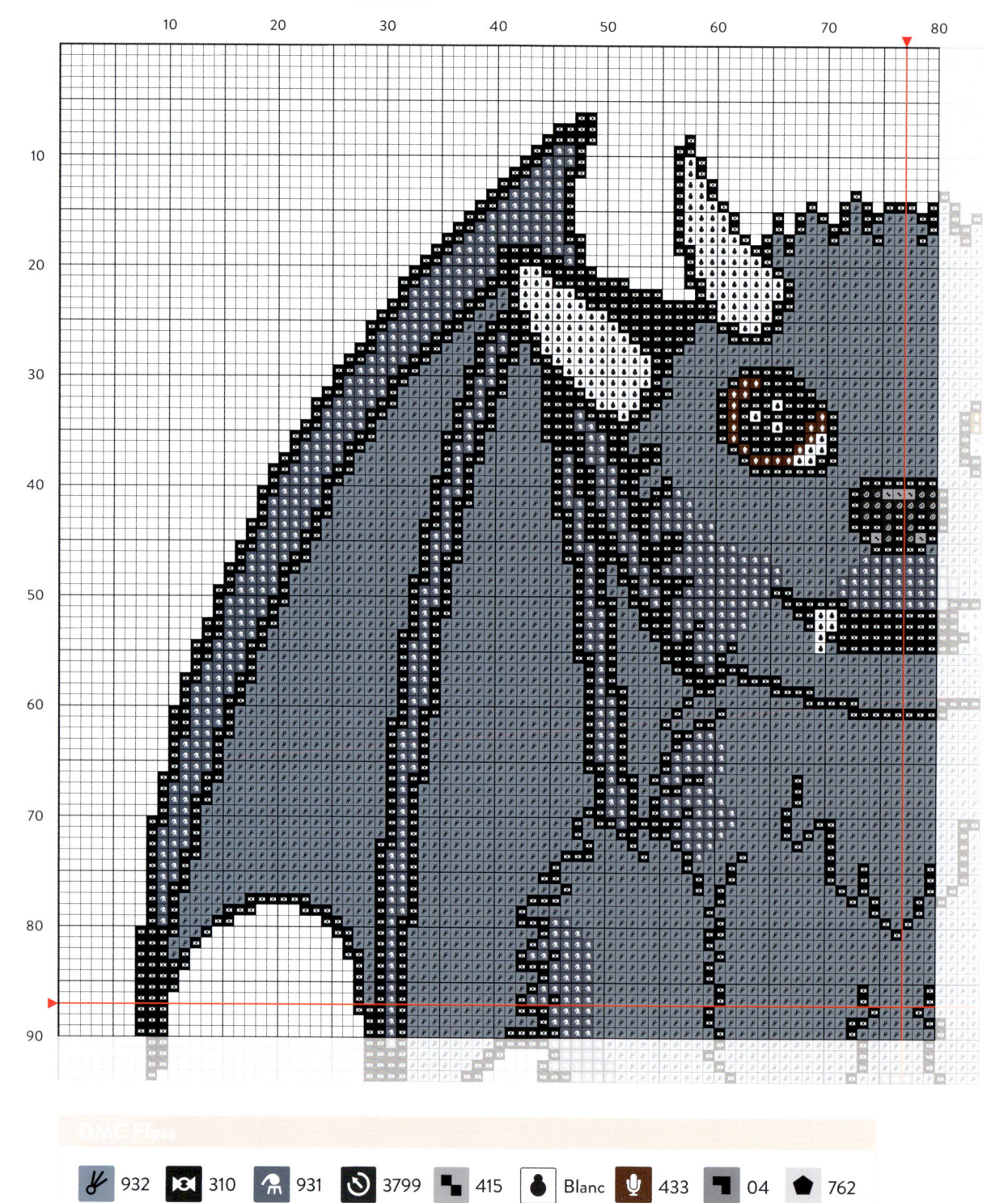

DMC Floss

932 | 310 | 931 | 3799 | 415 | Blanc | 433 | 04 | 762

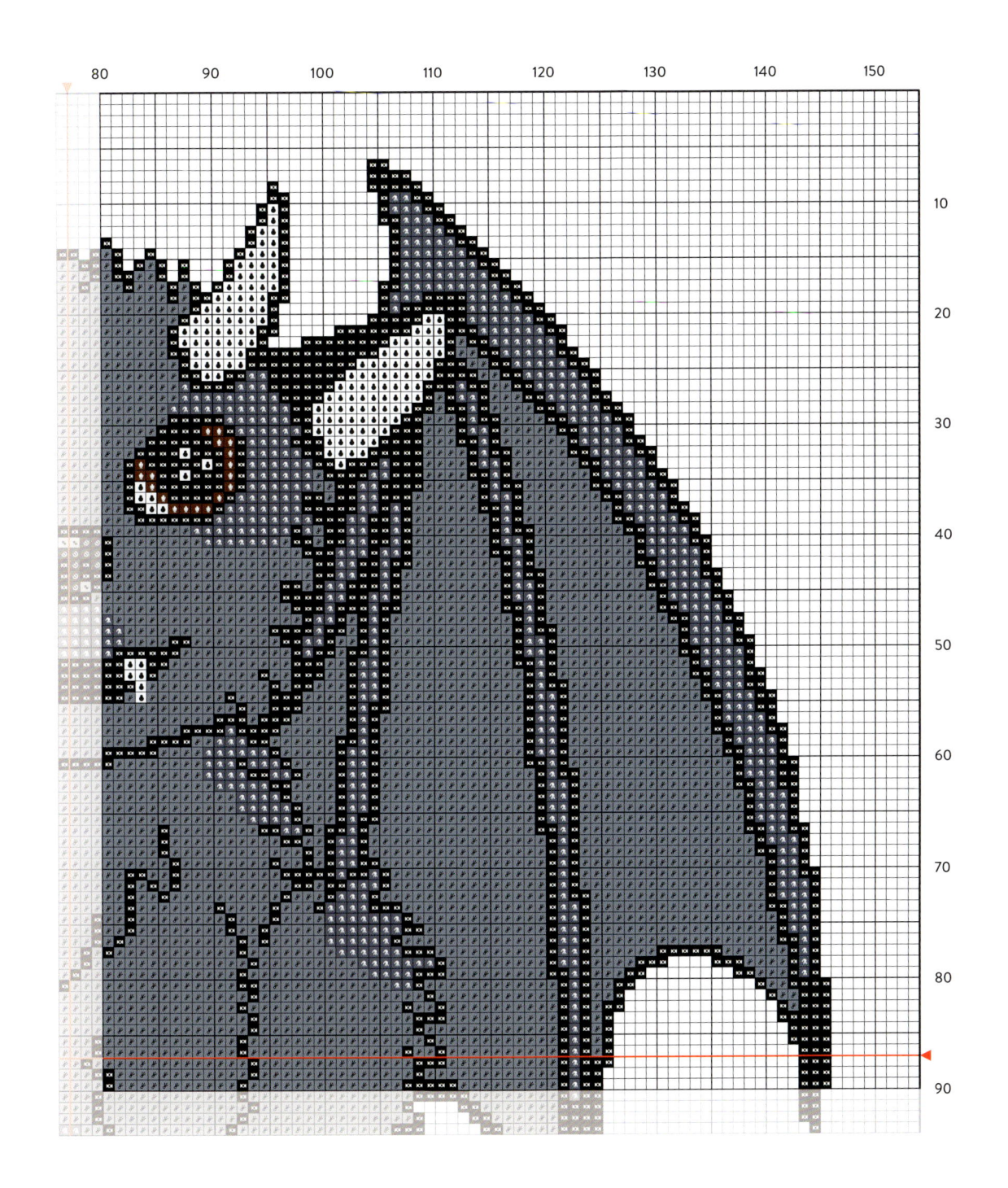

GARGOYLE Stitch Pattern, *continued*

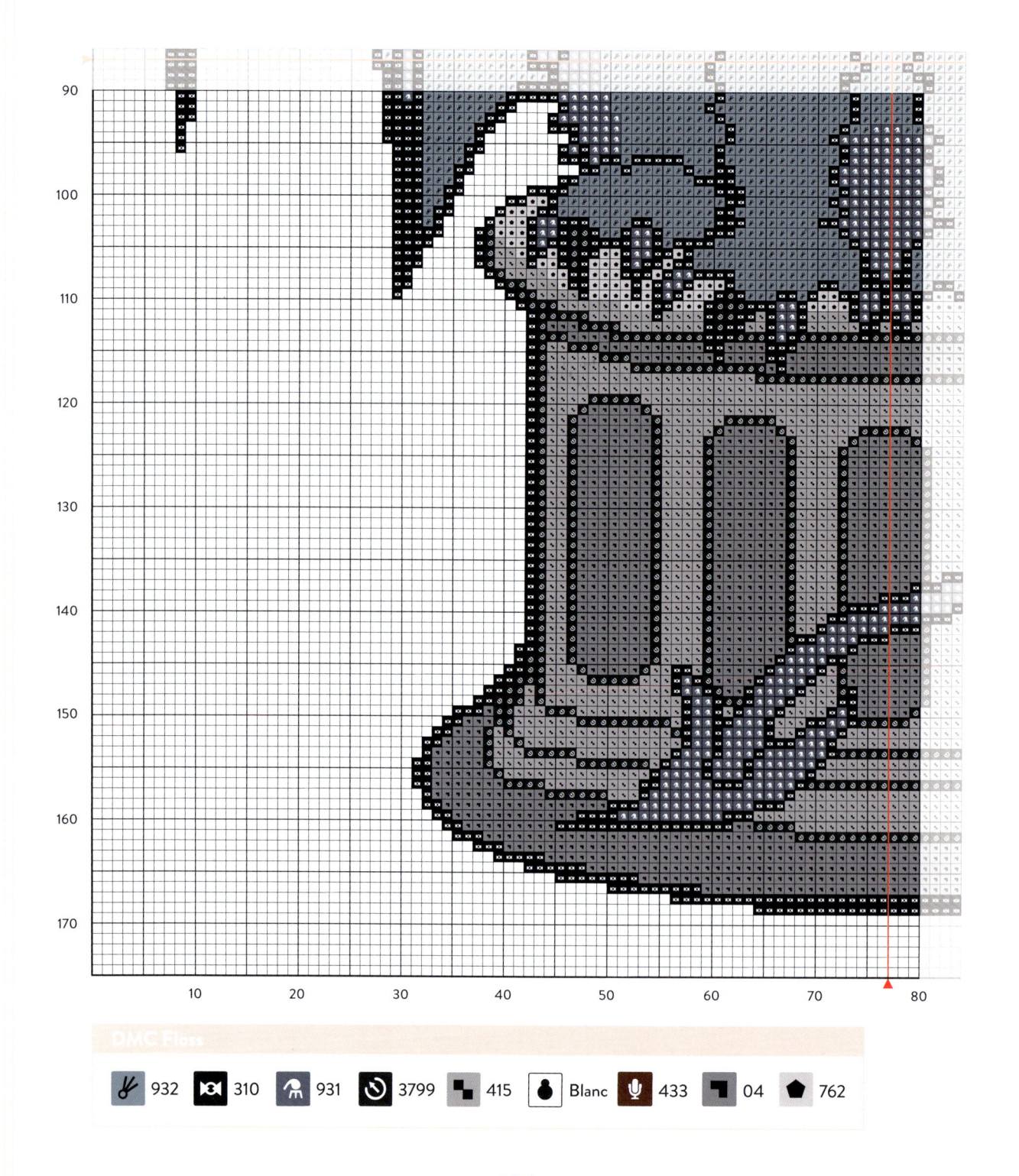

DMC Floss

932 | 310 | 931 | 3799 | 415 | Blanc | 433 | 04 | 762

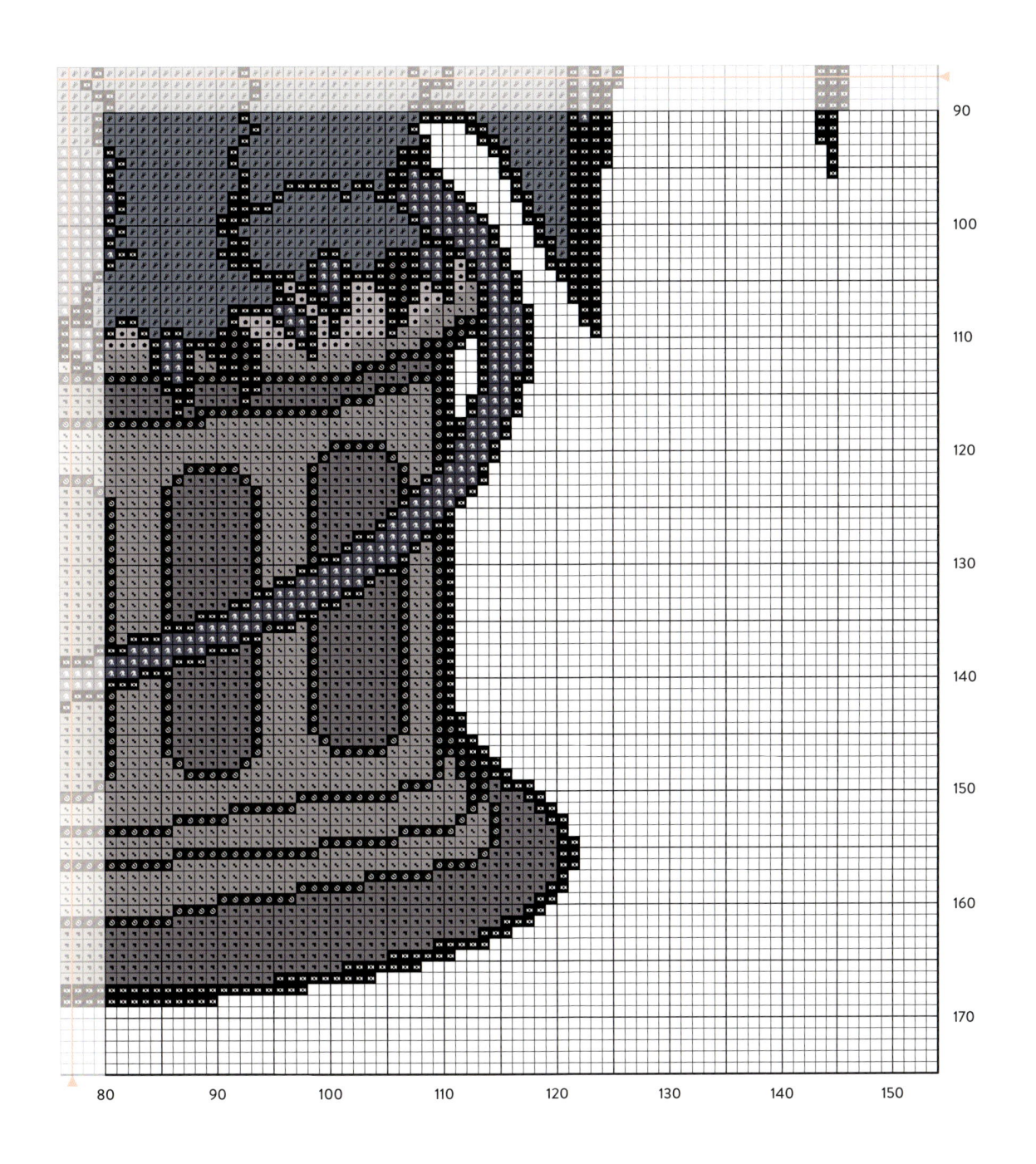

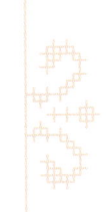

CTHULHU

NICKAME: Cthuuti

AGE: Great Old One

LOCATION: R'lyeh

HOBBIES: Being worshiped, waiting, dreaming, driving folks mad

First appearing in Lovecraft's "The Call of Cthulhu," published in 1928, the myth around the creature known as Cthulhu has been added to and expanded on for almost 100 years. He is a cosmic entity known as a Great Old One, and he's usually depicted as a massive scaly humanoid monster with large leathery wings and a bulbous head with giant tentacles descending from around his mouth. Cthulhu's worshipers are known to chant "Ph'nglui mglw'nafh Cthulhu R'lyeh wgah'nagl fhtagn," which translates to "In his house at R'lyeh, dead Cthulhu waits dreaming."

STRANDS USED:	2
AIDA COUNT:	14 (white)
HOOP SIZE:	5" (12.5 cm)
FINISHED SIZE:	4½" × 3½" (11.5 × 9 cm)
FRAMED SIZE:	5" × 5" (12.5 × 12.5 cm)

CTHULHU Stitch Pattern

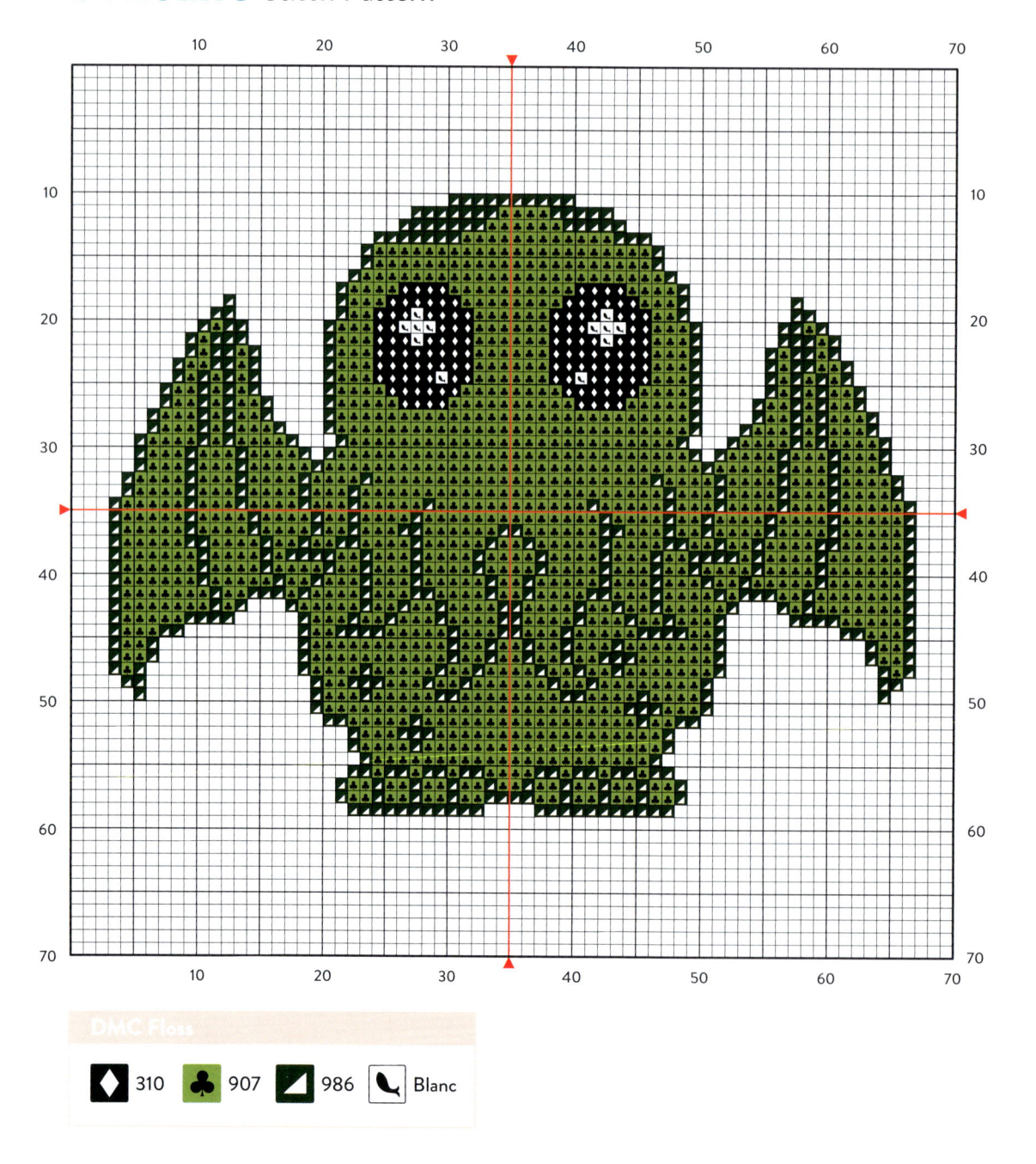

Above these apparent hieroglyphics was a figure of evidently pictorial intent, though its impressionistic execution forbade a very clear idea of its nature. It seemed to be a sort of monster, or symbol representing a monster, of a form which only a diseased fancy could conceive. If I say that my somewhat extravagant imagination yielded simultaneous pictures of an octopus, a dragon, and a human caricature, I shall not be unfaithful to the spirit of the thing.

—H. P. LOVECRAFT, "THE CALL OF CTHULHU"

Howard Phillips Lovecraft (1890–1937) is said to have given several contradictory accounts of how to properly pronounce "Cthulhu." He transcribed it most often as *Khlûl'-hloo.* However, according to some of Lovecraft's letters, since the word was created in an alien tongue, it is almost impossible for it to be pronounced correctly by humans. Which would mean that any way you may choose to say it, you're saying it wrong!

ACKNOWLEDGMENTS

I would like to thank my sister, April, without whom this book would not have been possible. Not only did she step up and write all the things, but she is my go-to for opinions and advice on my creature (and all other) designs.

Thank you to our mother and grandmother for teaching us cross-stitch, embroidery, and lots of other crafty things when we were kids. They, as well as our crafty aunts, also took us to local craft fairs where they would sell their handmade goods.

Thanks to everyone who has purchased cross-stitch kits and patterns from me in the past, and (in advance) all those who will purchase from me in the future. I hope you enjoy every bit of it!

I want to thank my model stitchers for their beautiful stitchwork in this book and elsewhere:

- April LaBranche
- Marsha LaBranche
- Victoria Wisinski
- Lily Stricklin
- Jen Hogan
- Caitlin "Cat" Booth
- Leia Verner
- Caroline Schleimer
- Deanna Simmons

A huge thank-you to our editor, Sandra Korinchak, and Schiffer Craft Publishing for guiding us through this process and making it all within reach.

Thank you to my brother-in-law, Jason, for nudging April, who in turn nudged me, to get the work done.

And finally, thank you to all our family and friends who have supported us and Spot Colors over the years.

Nicole LaBranche